MONAGI
FOLK
TALES

Best wishes
John Kelly

2017

MONAGHAN
FOLK
TALES

STEVE LALLY

The
History
Press
Ireland

This book is dedicated to

My uncle Donal O'Donoghue, 1928–2017.
'Thank you for all your encouragement.'

My friend Ray Dunne, 1981–2016.
'Till we meet again on Raglan Road.'

Patrick Kavanagh, 1904–1967.
'I went down to Co. Monaghan after fifty years
or so, and I enquired what you were like to know …'

First published 2017

The History Press Ireland
50 City Quay
Dublin 2
Ireland
www.thehistorypress.ie

The History Press Ireland is a member of Publishing Ireland,
the Irish book publishers' association.

© Steve Lally, 2017
Illustrations © Steve Lally, 2017
Patrick Kavanagh illustration © James Patrick Ryan, 2017

The right of Steve Lally, to be identified as the Author
of this work has been asserted in accordance with the
Copyright, Designs and Patents Act 1988.

British Library Cataloguing in Publication Data.
A catalogue record for this book is available from the British Library.

ISBN 978 1 84588 521 2

Printed and bound by CPI Group
Typesetting and origination by The History Press

CONTENTS

FOREWORD

Stories have formed part of my life for as long as I can remember and so too have the people who told them. Some of my earliest memories are of my mother weaving her tales beside the fire in the front room of our house before my brother and I went to bed. She had the gift of being able to turn everyday occurrences from our lives into tales of excitement and wonder. When we lived on Dublin Street in Monaghan, my older brother Michael, then aged 3, got lost for an hour and was safely found. In a different home, this might have been an unremarkable incident, but in our house, my mother turned it into a drama full of excitement and adventure:

> Well, I was up the walls with worry and had the whole town out looking for him. He wasn't in the yard and he wasn't on the street. I was afraid he might have fallen into the canal in Old Cross Square, but there was no sign of him there. I met two young guards and they said they would search Glaslough Street and Park Street. Then suddenly I thought of Peter's Lake. He was always a devil for playing with water so I went around there as quickly as I could. My heart was in my mouth and all the time I was thinking surely he couldn't have got that far and Sacred Heart of Jesus let nothing have happened to him. When I got to the lake, there was my brave Michael with a stick in his hand and one of the guards leading him away from the water. 'You'd want to keep an eye on that young fella missus,' he said, as if I didn't know already. There were two beautiful white swans on the lake and Michael was waving the stick

at them and shouting at me excitedly, 'See a gucks, mammy, see a gucks!'

We would clamour for more and an incident in one tale would lead to another tale. Michael mistaking the swans for ducks might lead her to the story of 'The Ugly Duckling' or it might lead her to tell us the story of the 'Children of Lir', one of the most heartbreaking of Ireland's ancient legends, which, along with 'The Quest of the Sons of Tuirenn' and 'The Fate of the Sons of Uisneach', is one of the three sorrows of storytelling.

Looking back, I realise that my mother had the same gift that the poet Patrick Kavanagh identified in his poem 'Epic'. She could make an *Iliad* from the bric-a-brac of incident and accident accumulated over the course of ordinary family life. She made me realise that our local stories could be every bit as interesting, heartbreaking, fascinating and funny as any myth or legend, once they were told in the right way.

For a long time, however, I didn't think that what we had in Monaghan was interesting. As a child at school, there were no great 'A-list' Monaghan heroes to read about in the history books. The county boasted no major historical sites of national significance. We had no Newgrange or Tara, no major rivers, no major lakes, no mighty mountains, no towns of note. Our local village was called after the patron saint of the mentally afflicted, St Dympna, and that wasn't much to talk about in the days when mental health issues were taboo. Besides, she wasn't in the same league as St Patrick, St Brigid or St Colmcille. Furthermore, Monaghan didn't feature in any Irish myths or legends and rarely or barely could a single photo of Monaghan scrape its way into any of the tourist books full of images of Ireland.

I really did begin to wonder if County Monaghan had a story to tell. As I grew older, I started to consider all the tales I had heard. My mother, father, uncles, aunts, friends, neighbours and other outstanding local characters had all contributed to my store. My age was still in single figures when I heard the late Peter McKenna of Annahagh tell the story of the man who built his house on the fairy path out near the mountain. Peter's voice continues to echo in my head over forty years later, saying 'Dip the finger and not the thumb' and assuring his listeners that the story was true by confiding that he had 'seen with his very own eyes' the turf the hero drew home from the bog in the donkey and cart he had magically captured in the tale.

I remembered my father telling us about Skelton's Inn and the Ghost Dog of Tydavnet, my Uncle Patsy giving me 'The Tale of Cricket McKenna' and 'John Martha and the Landlord's Gold', and Leo Lord sending a shiver down my spine as he described how he had seen the head of St Dympna on the ground at the back of Tydavnet Chapel. I knew Peter Smyth, a man whose life had started in the Monaghan workhouse and ended without the price of a funeral, but whose headstone was erected by his friends and neighbours. They recalled him fondly in our locality with stories about his singing ability and his legendary wit. And I knew that among all this material, there was indeed something of interest to tell.

Some of the tales I have gathered are to be found within the pages of this book and all credit for that goes to Steve Lally. Steve is not only the author, but an extremely gifted storyteller. I first heard him at an event organised by the Storytellers of Ireland in 2016. He captivated an adult audience and drew us into the hilarious and bizarre adventure of the Pooka Horse of Rathcoffey. (Rathcoffey is the Kildare townland where Lally grew up. This story can be found in the Irish History Press publication *Kildare Folk Tales*, another book in this series.) Reading the story is fun, but listening to Steve tell it is an experience to treasure.

Whether he realises it or not, Steve may be making a little bit of history. *Monaghan Folk Tales* could be one of the last books to contain some uncollected tales transcribed from local lore. Most of the tales I passed on to Steve were given to me by people who had heard them before the advent of electricity and television. They come from the last generation to experience storytelling as an everyday art form and a chief means of entertainment.

So good luck to all who read this book. Enjoy the stories and please tell them to someone else. You never know the impact a simple story might have on the imagination of a child or the loneliness that can be alleviated by sharing a tale with another.

Francis McCarron, April 2017

ACKNOWLEDGEMENTS

I would like to thank the following for their help in writing this book:

Paula Flynn, my soulmate and oracle to 'The Good Folk'; Isabella and Woody, who fire my imagination with their stories; Francis McCarron, fellow storyteller and new found friend; Brian Dooley, an inspiration and wealth of knowledge; Danny Aughey, with plenty of stories under his hat; Dan Kerr, a sharp memory and a soft word; Deirdriu McQuaid, a great support; Everyone at Castle Leslie, thank you; Patrick McCabe, thanks for pointing us in the right direction; Johnny Madden, thank you for your help and enthusiasm; Pat O'Neill, thanks for sharing your stories; Patsy and Linda Boylan, for introducing us to the fairies of Monaghan; Doreen McBride, thanks for the books; Liz Weir, for all your support as always; everyone at the Patrick Kavanagh Centre; Fergal Lally, for his help researching; James Patrick Ryan, for immortalising the great poet in your art; UCD Irish Folklore Commission; Monaghan, Clones, Banbridge and DKIT Library.

INTRODUCTION

When I took on the task of writing this book in 2016, I had no idea what sort of experience I would be having. Little did I know that I was about to embark on a great journey of adventure and wonder.

In his book, *The Green Fool*, Patrick Kavanagh goes stumbling into Fairyland, when he only intended to go visit a friend beyond the Hill of Mullacrew. I too stumbled into a strange world where I was to meet all sorts of characters and visit many places that would both enlighten and enthral.

It all began when I headed off with my partner, Paula Flynn, to visit Patrick Kavanagh's grave in Inniskeen. I had just put in a proposal for *Monaghan Folk Tales* with The History Press and when we got to the resting place of the great poet I asked him if he would put in a good word for me. That evening, when we went home, I checked my emails and there it was … I had got the contract to write the book and it really felt that I had gotten the blessing of Kavanagh himself.

So I embarked on my journey. I travelled through the countryside, along the wee roads and lanes, through the townlands, villages and towns of County Monaghan. As I did, I met with so many people who helped me along the way. I imagined myself like Kavanagh on the ass and cart, not knowing where he was going, hoping that his mother's wisdom and the ass's natural instincts would take him to where he was going and get him back safely.

As I travelled along the roads on the old ass and cart, out of the mist came my brother Fergal and in his hand was a book he had bought for me on Kavanagh. He stated that he hoped it would help on my journey and he wished me well. I thanked him and he disappeared into the shadows.

As I trundled along I found myself in the town of Clones, outside the magnificent new library there. I went inside, it was familiar to me, as I had performed stories to local schools there before. I met with Deirdriu McQuaid, Senior Executive Librarian, who gave me a list of people that I should talk to, and also I collected some valuable research material. Thanking her, I loaded the books on to the old cart and the donkey sniffed the air as if it knew exactly where to go next.

I was taken to the house of Dan Kerr, who lives in Clones town. Dan is a man of 96 years but has all his mind and spirit about him. He made me feel welcome with homemade cake and cups of tae. He spoke about the railways, smuggling, the GAA and how he had worked on the buses when he was a young man. He also spoke of a memorable passenger, Patrick Kavanagh, and he had some lovely stories about him. I thanked Dan and headed on, making sure to bring some water and a bit of grub for the poor ass that waited patiently outside.

Next, I found myself outside Collins Barracks, Dublin. Inside there was an AGM of The Storytellers of Ireland, and there was a talk being given by Katherine Soutar Caddick, the lady who would be creating the cover of this very book. At the meeting I met a man called Francis McCarron, who is a fine storyteller from Tydavnet, County Monaghan. He shared many fantastical tales about the good folk and strange characters of County Monaghan, some of which are included in this book. I bid him farewell and headed off on the auld ass and cart, but I was to see Francie again in both Monaghan town and Castleblayney and each time I was able to pile the auld cart up with lots of stories and anecdotes from his home county.

When I was in Dublin the auld ass brought me out to University College Dublin (UCD) where I met with Críostóir Mac Cárthaigh the archivist of the National Folklore Collection. He introduced me to the children who had gathered stories, myths, legends, songs, poems and a whole plethora of other traditions and pastimes from their families, friends and neighbours over eighty years ago.

They had some great stories, indeed; I thanked them and as a reward I let them all have a go on the auld ass and cart and shure the auld donkey was delighted with all the attention and praise he was getting from the children. As I loaded up the auld cart with their stories and told them that I would say hello to their children's children and their children too when I got back to Co. Monaghan.

Then the ass took me to the Westenra Arms Hotel in Monaghan town. The beast grunted and snorted, directing me to go inside. So in I went and sitting in the foyer, waiting for me, was Danny Aughey. He welcomed me with a big warm smile and a firm handshake. We sat in the hotel, where he told me some great stories of ghostly encounters and some funny tales of smuggling. Afterwards I thanked him and he gave me a package of tales to smuggle back with me across the border. I hid them in the old cart and was on my way again.

But I did not always travel alone, for my partner Paula would come along with me and suggest a few places to stop off at along the way. These included Johnny Madden of Hilton Park, a stately home in County Monaghan, and the writer Pat McCabe, both of whom were very helpful in pointing me in the right direction.

Whilst travelling around County Monaghan we got to see many of its hidden treasures, such as the breathtaking set of original Harry Clarke stained-glass windows at St Joseph's Church in Carrickmacross, Tydavnet Cemetery and Errigal Truagh medieval church and graveyard, and that's where we made sure to avoid the gaze of the Graveyard Bride.

The donkey took us to Glaslough and brought us to Castle Leslie, where we met Sammy Leslie who kindly welcomed us inside. We were shown around the castle and tken to see its archives, which proved to be a fascinating experience. After our visit I was contacted by Tarka King, the grandson of Shane Leslie, who very kindly offered to include some of his late grandfather's fine poetry into this book.

The cart was starting to get quite full of stories and passengers at this stage. There were ghosts, fairies, a banshee and some very unsavoury characters such as Joe Fee and Skelton the Innkeeper. But we also had the gentle and tragic Wilde Sisters, the Three Faithful Dogs and, in the middle of it all, St Davnet, keeping everybody calm and at ease.

But there was someone missing … Of course, where was Paddy Kavanagh? Well, now the auld ass knew exactly where to go. In an instant we were in Inniskeen at The Patrick Kavanagh Centre, which was re-opening its doors after the long winter. Paula and I left the auld ass outside who was more than happy to be back home in Inniskeen.

Inside we met many great characters, including those who run the centre, and we were given a tour of the place, which was very impressive indeed. I was then introduced to Brian Dooley of

Inniskeen who wasted no time, hopping on the ass and cart with us and taking us about Inniskeen and Mucker, showing us all the places associated with the great poet.

We even stopped off along the way at Billy Brennan's Barn for a wee dance. We waved Brian off as we helped Paddy Kavanagh onto the cart along with the assistance of a few of his friends, such as Red Pat and of course a couple of the Lennons and Cassidys.

Then the ass took us to see Patsy Boylan and his daughter Linda who live in Inniskeen. They showed us their land with the fairy field and fairy fort upon it. Patsy and Linda had some great fairy stories and a few tales about Kavanagh too, who was now roaring abuse at auld Skelton the Innkeeper for his poor service.

I had spent a long time trying to imagine what these people, places and characters looked like so I took this once-in-a-lifetime opportunity to illustrate them as they congregated on the old cart.

My old friend James Patrick Ryan from Limerick showed up to do the drawing of Paddy, for which I was only delighted, as Paddy had now fallen out with Joe Fee and was trying to get a race going with the three dogs. Well, James did a great job and I feel he captured the very essence of Kavanagh in his drawing.

Paula had played a huge part on this journey and as we travelled together we often found ourselves lost in a wonderful world of mystery, imagination and magic. We laughed at how the auld ass always knew its way back so there was never any need to worry about maps and satnavs and we remembered how Paddy had told us that the ass is a blessed animal. We both watched as the ass walked away with its cargo of passengers and how they disappeared into the mist, but we were not sad for we knew that their stories would live on in this wee book.

Overall it was an amazing experience and I have collected so many wonderful stories, songs and poems. Some are terrifying, some funny and some are heartbreaking but all of them are magical in their own way and capture the essence of County Monaghan. I did not encounter the stony grey soil that Kavanagh wrote about but a rich landscape of myth, legend and human experience whose stories are worthy of any collection of folklore.

Steve Lally, May 2017

1

PATRICK KAVANAGH: WORDS OF EARTH AND CLAY

Ever since I was first introduced to the poetry of Patrick Kavanagh by my father when I was a child, then listening to my uncle Donal O'Donoghue talk about the poet, I have been captivated by the words and imagery in Kavanagh's poems. Some are beautiful and some are frightening. All of them are sublime. He created images full of darkness and despair and yet out of this he could create visions of sheer utopian bliss. He saw complexity and depth in the simplest of things and he could turn an ordinary event into a saga of epic proportions. His words were his power and in this he was all-powerful.

But he was also a shy and awkward man who seemed to feel like an outsider. The local people in his community of Inniskeen were either wary and sceptical of him or saw him as a figure of ridicule and absurdity. When he moved to Dublin, he was seen as a backward, even primitive, man by the literary elite. It was only in his later years and after his death that people really began to appreciate the absolute and unique genius of Patrick Kavanagh.

In Kavanagh's poem 'If you ever go to Dublin town', he requests that if you go to the capital city in a hundred years or so, to inquire about him and to ask what he was like. Well, it so happens that this year, 2017, is the fiftieth anniversary of Kavanagh's death in 1967, and so I went down to Co. Monaghan and availed myself of the opportunity to speak to many people who knew or had met Kavanagh in his lifetime.

I have put together a collection of their anecdotes and memories of this eccentric, brilliant, yet troubled man.

The works of Patrick Kavanagh created their own unique folklore, giving a weight and mythic quality to ordinary people and places. Places such as 'Raglan Road', 'Shancoduff', 'Gardiner Street' and 'Billy Brennan's barn' were given a resonance comparable to that of *Tír na nÓg*, the ancient Celtic land of youth, 'Mount Olympus', the ancient Greek home of the gods, Hades, the ancient Greek land of the dead, and Heorot, the mead hall of the Danish King Hrothgar. Locals like 'Old McCabe' and the Duffys have the same heroic stature as Odysseus and the Trojans from Homer's *Iliad*.

Fifty years after his death, these places and people still call to mind the gods, warriors and sacred realms of Kavanagh's work.

Patrick Kavanagh once said, 'A poet is never one of the people. He is detached, remote, and the life of small-time dances and talk about football would not be for him. He might take part but could not belong.' This was very true of Patrick Kavanagh and when I spoke to the people of Co. Monaghan who knew him, it became even more apparent that he had been an outsider.

The first person I spoke to was Dan Kerr of Clones. Despite being 96 years old, he looks like the picture of health and has a spark in his eye that lets you know that he is still sharp as a pin. Back in the 1940s and '50s, when he was working on the buses in Monaghan, Kavanagh was one of his regular passengers. He said that he would take Kavanagh on trips from Inniskeen to Dublin, making regular stops along the way at various pubs that Kavanagh liked to frequent, though on other occasions, Dan was told to avoid these pubs and go to different ones instead. This was because he was often barred from the pubs, but usually he would be absolved of his misdemeanours, and allowed back in.

Dan got on well with Kavanagh and saw beyond his rough exterior. Even back then, he recognised the genius of the poet and was a great admirer of his work. Dan had not only met and spent time with Kavanagh; he also knew the 'The Navvy Poet' Patrick MacGill from Glenties in Donegal and was a great admirer of his work too.

Dan said that when Kavanagh was riding the buses, people gave him a wide berth as they were unsure of what sort of greeting they would get. He was known to take newspapers from other passengers if he was feeling bored by the journey and would make all sorts of smart comments to those who had the misfortune of catching his gaze when he was in one of his less jovial moods. He would often ask people if they were looking at the horns on his head. But Dan knew that there was a softer side to Kavanagh and realised that the poet's rough exterior was a way for him to protect himself from the cruel and judgemental world of the old conservative Catholic Ireland.

But it was not all negative. Dan talked about the big laugh Kavanagh had and how he enjoyed a song, a good joke or a witty story and was often great company on the bus journeys.

Another man I met who knew Kavanagh was Danny Aughey from Glaslough. We met at the Westenra Hotel in Monaghan town. He wore a tweed hat and jacket and had an air of the country gentleman about him. He recounted that although Kavanagh was a spiritual man, he was often at odds with the teachings of the Catholic Church.

He shared a lovely wee story with me about how Paddy would regularly cough and fidget during Mass, which would in turn put the priest off his sermon. So on one particular Sunday, when Paddy was sitting at the back of the church during Mass, coughing and shuffling about the place, the auld priest decided that he had had enough of him and asked him to leave as he was disturbing his sermon.

So Paddy, bold as brass, got up and walked right up to the top of the church and, out loud in front of all the congregation, he said, 'I will go, for I can get more about God from the bits and pieces of everyday living, instead of listening to your voice rising and falling like a briar blowing in the wind.' With that, Kavanagh walked out of the church, leaving in his wake a stunned priest and his bewildered flock. Kavanagh was very much his own man. He saw things how they were and did not try to brush over hypocrisy or injustice of any kind with words of conformity.

Well, I knew that if I wanted to hear first-hand stories about Kavanagh, I would have to go back to where it all started, in his home town of Inniskeen in Co. Monaghan. Inniskeen (which means 'Peaceful Island') is a pleasant little village in south Monaghan, bordering Louth and Armagh.

Paula and I went to the re-opening of the Kavanagh Centre in March of this year. We had the pleasure of meeting lots of interesting characters, listening to their stories about Kavanagh and listening to people reciting his poetry.

While we were there, we were introduced to a tall and striking gentleman named Brian Dooley. Now, his name rang a bell with me as several people I had spoken to had mentioned this man, saying that he was a great source of information about Monaghan and a great admirer of Patrick Kavanagh's work.

Brian was very friendly indeed and when I asked him if he would tell me some stories from Monaghan's folklore, he was only too happy to oblige. So we arranged to meet again. He also took

me to meet Pat O'Neill, who told me the terrible tale of the Wild
Goose Lodge in Co. Louth.

Afterwards I asked Brian about the poet Patrick Kavanagh and
what he had been like. He explained to me that Kavanagh had
lived at a time when people were suspicious of writers and poets,
for to have your name in the paper was considered to be a terrible
thing. Before Kavanagh there was another local poet called John
McEnaney (1872–1943), the 'Bard of Callenberg' (Callenberg
is a townland just outside of Inniskeen). When Kavanagh began
writing verse at about the age of 12 or so, McEnaney was retiring
from verse. McEnaney was a man with a fierce tongue, which he
was ready to use as a weapon in rhyme on the slightest annoyance.
People would also go to McEnaney if they wanted to get revenge
on someone who had slighted them. They would give McEnaney
the details and he would in turn compose a poisonous ballad. As
a result, no one in the area trusted a poet, as they were afraid of a
cruel verse being composed about them.

There is a great story about a local fellow who wanted a poisonous ballad written about his neighbours, so he went to Kavanagh's
house. He knocked on the door and when it opened, he asked
if this was the poet's house. Kavanagh replied, 'You're looking at
him.' So your man went about, giving Kavanagh all the details of
the bunch of devils that were his neighbours and how he wished
for their souls to burn on the slabs of hell for all eternity, et cetera.

Well, he was getting very excited until he asked Kavanagh what
he wanted in exchange for these damning words, and Kavanagh
quoted him a price per line and explained that a poet can't live
on air alone. Now, the man was not too happy with this fee at all,
so he decided to leave and as he was leaving he shouted back at
Kavanagh, 'I'm off over the hill to see Auld McEnaney, he'll rhyme
the be-jaysus out of ya for thruppence a line!'

Going right back to ancient Ireland, the bards had great power
and they were revered and feared by royalty and peasantry alike,
for they could make or break you with what they said about you.
If a bard wanted to ruin your name, they would compose an *ail
bréthre* (a verbal insult) and this, in turn, would be what you were
remembered for, as the bard would recite the damning poem in
public wherever they went on their travels.

In my second book of Irish folklore, *Kildare Folk Tales*, you can find the story of 'Queen Buan', which features the cruel druid/ bard Atherne (the court bard of King Conor Mac Nessa, the High King of Ulster), who caused terrible bloodshed through his vengeful ballads.

Because most folk in Kavanagh's time could not read or write as education was very limited, it was very much part of the psyche that one should not trust a poet or writer. Although it was well known in Inniskeen that Kavanagh was writing poetry, no one would mention it unless they wanted to get a rise out of one of Kavanagh's siblings. 'Your brother's a bard!' would be insult enough.

So Kavanagh's status as a poet did not do him any favours and people treated him with suspicion and even contempt, for a poet was a dangerous thing. Sadly they did not perceive his great ability for painting beautiful pictures with his words.

But Kavanagh did try to fit in, in his own way, for he always wanted to be part of the craic with the other lads from his townland of Mucker, who were the Lennons and Cassidys (they feature in his poetry). Now, these were all fine, big, fit fellows, who were great footballers and farmers with a sense of fun and mischief about them and many of them had taken part in the Irish War of Independence. Kavanagh was no great farmer and certainly no soldier, but he was a great goalkeeper and played for the local team and this is probably how he ingratiated himself with these local lads.

Kavanagh looked up to them greatly, but he was not like them and longed terribly to be part of their world. He said that he felt like 'a stranger within the walls' when he was in their company, but Kavanagh still insisted on spending time with these tough but genuine characters.

He would go with them to meetings held by the Department of Agriculture at local schools, where advice would be given to farmers on how to improve their produce and husbandry practices on their farms. Now, the sole purpose of the young Kavanagh and the Lennon and Cassidy boys was to interrupt these meetings, which they saw as a bit of craic. On one occasion, Kavanagh and his crew showed up at one of these meetings as the instructor was explaining what to do if a large object like a potato got stuck in a cow's throat. He explained that you need to get a piece of wood to hold open the beast's mouth, then you stick your arm down the animal's throat in order to retrieve the spud and prevent the animal from choking. Kavanagh saw this as a golden opportunity to have a laugh at the instructor's expense and asked him what type of wood would he recommend. The instructor innocently went about telling Paddy the shape and size of the piece of wood to use. Midway through this, Kavanagh blurts out, 'Would the shaft of a cart be any good?' This, of course, was followed by a big guffaw from the Lennons and Cassidys, much to the satisfaction of Kavanagh and the annoyance of the instructor.

On another occasion, the instructor was talking about how to go about growing barley, but Monaghan is not a barley county as the soil is too heavy. Well, there was a farmer there who was interested in growing barley and he asked what sort of soil was needed. He was told that he needed at least 6 inches of good light soil. But this man lived in a particularly rocky part of Monaghan and Kavanagh knew him, so when the instructor told him about the good soil, Kavanagh shouted over at him, 'Well, you would be wasting your time there now!'

After hearing these stories about Kavanagh from Brian, I thanked him and we arranged to meet again at a later date, which we did.

Brian then took it upon himself to show me around Inniskeen and point out some of the places featured in Kavanagh's most famous and loved works. He suggested that I drive around Inniskeen, so he could show me the sights. As we drove out of Brian's driveway, I listened as he pointed out those black hills that Kavanagh had described as his Alps, where he climbed his Matterhorn to bring a sheaf of hay to three starving calves, and there I saw the 'rushy beards' of Shancoduff.

We went to the house in the townland of Mucker (meaning 'The Place of the Pigs') where Kavanagh was born in 1904. It is a fine-looking house with green painted doors and windows set into its grey stone walls. I stood outside the gate, where Kavanagh's father once played the melodeon, and I imagined his mother outside milking the cows. As I observed the green painted door, I could not help looking for those six nicks carved on the doorpost by a small child over a hundred years ago.

It was strange to see the bins outside the front of the house, with the name 'KAVANAGH' spray-painted down the side of each one. I imagined Paddy shuffling out the side door with a bag of rubbish, cursing about separating the organic from the recycling.

On the other side of the road stood Cassidy's hanging hill. I looked for the 'three whin bushes' riding across the horizon like the 'Three Wise Kings' from Kavanagh's childhood imagination.

As we drove along the little winding roads and lanes, Brian recited Kavanagh's poetry in his strong Monaghan accent, bringing what I saw before me to life and giving greater depth and meaning to the poems I had known since childhood.

After we left Kavanagh's house, we went on to Kednaminsha National School, the school attended by Kavanagh, where he was taught by Miss Cassidy. I was told that on his first day at school, Kavanagh escaped and ran and hid under the nearby bridge. His mother was up in arms when she found out he was missing. There was not much the teacher could do with him for he was not that interested as a student, but he showed great signs of intelligence and could read from a very young age. Miss Cassidy had said that it would be great if he could go on to secondary school in Carrickmacross, but this was not to be as his family had no money. He left school at 13 to work with his father as a shoemaker.

As time went on, Kavanagh wanted to prove his independence, so he saved whatever money he had and bought himself a horse, which he referred to as 'The Kicking Mare'.

Now, Kavanagh was not great when it came to working the land, nor was he great with animals for that matter, and when he went to the fair at Carrickmacross (known as Carrick) he was sold a dinger. He bought a horse that had spent its life as a brewery horse, drawing kegs of beer about Carrick and Dundalk. This horse had always worked by itself and did not want to work alongside another one, pulling a plough. So it would kick and rear up whenever Kavanagh tried to harness it to the swing-trees of a plough.

Now, at the time, the local farmers had a thing going that they called 'a swap'. This meant that if you had a plough but no horse you could lend it to someone who needed one, and in return they would lend you their horse. But as Kavanagh's horse was so unruly, no one wanted to work with him and this only enhanced Kavanagh's sense of isolation from his fellows.

On hearing these stories, I started to see why Kavanagh lost himself in the world that he had created through his poetry and writing, even changing the names of well-known landmarks that he had grown up with, including changing the name of Inniskeen to Dargan in *Tarry Flynn*.

He could not fit into the world around him, but, like the ship-wrecked castaway Alexander Selkirk, he was king and ruler of his own world, which he had created himself.

Kavanagh's spirit was all around and I was on a fantastic adventure through his world. I was directed up winding lanes and roads until I came to the place where the bicycles would go by in twos and threes.

Yes, indeed, I was going to Billy Brennan's barn. Climbing over the gate I made my way up to the old barn. I walked around the barn, with the sun shining brightly and the sound of birdsong all around. I tried to imagine what it would have been like to have gone to a dance there all those years ago. I was told stories of how when the floorboards sprung with the dancing, the hens would be bounced up and down on their roost. When all this was going on the local parish priest would be cursing the whole affair and pulling girls off their partners' laps and separating dancers who were getting too close to each other by using his cane.

I could imagine the sounds, smells and music that permeated the old barn, with its whitewashed stone walls, red windows and doors, with a good-luck horseshoe hanging over the main door. And I could envision Kavanagh alone, like Alexander Selkirk, standing at the top of the side steps, having a solitary cigarette or waiting outside, trying to muster the courage to go in and leave his solitary kingdom behind.

Leaving behind the legendary barn, I was then taken to what looked like an old cement shed in a place called Mullagh, which is an abbreviation for 'Mullahinsa'. Kavanagh mentions Mullahinsa in his poem 'Stony Grey Soil' and indeed this building was very stony and grey.

It was explained to me that in 1935, the government brought out the Dance Halls Act. This Act, made by the Oireachtas, enforced a licensing system and taxation on admission tickets. It also enforced a regulation on any dancing 'which is open to the public and in which persons present are entitled to participate actively' and applies broadly not just to pubs and clubs but to any 'place' defined as 'a building (including part of a building), yard, garden or other enclosed place, whether roofed or not roofed and whether the enclosure and the roofing (if any) are permanent or temporary'. The Act was introduced because the dances were seen as illegal, unsafe and ungodly. They had been taking place in old barns and sheds around the country and could not be monitored in any shape or form.

In 1932, there was a report from the Carrigan Commission on 'Juvenile Sex Crimes'. It was the same Carrigan report that decided the age of consent and banned the use of contraception in Ireland. This is what their report had to say about the dance halls:

> In the course of the Inquiry no form of abuse was blamed more persistently for pernicious consequences than the unlicensed dances held all over the country in unsuitable buildings and surroundings, for the profit of persons who are liable to no control or supervision by any authority. The scandals that are the outcome of such a situation are notorious. They have been denounced in pastorals, exposed in the Press, and condemned by clergy, judges and justices, without avail. Before us the Commissioner, speaking for the Civic Guard, said these dance gatherings in many districts were turned into 'orgies of dissipation, which in the present state of legislation the police are powerless to prevent.' In short, there is no effective legislation to put down this nuisance.

At the time, there was a parish priest called Bernard McGuire. Now, Father McGuire had been a lecturer in the ecclesiastical college in Salamanca, Spain. After many years in Spain, he was given the opportunity to be the parish priest in Inniskeen. Some saw this as a promotion from lecturing in sunny Spain, but more saw it as a demotion. He was parish priest in Inniskeen from 1916 to 1948. He was a staunch republican and a very strong-willed man.

He was very much against all of the dance hall malarkey and was furious when Mullagh Hall was built and financed in 1939 by a group of local men who had decided to take it upon themselves to create such a venue. This was done because the previous year it had been stated that if the hall was built using state funds, it would be under the sole control of the clergy and the lads were having none of it.

The men involved were Jemmy Kirk and John Lennon of Mucker (these men decided to build the hall as a private venture), Jemmy Huighie Meagan (who put up the land), Packie Duffy (who put up the money) and Tom Ruddy (who built it).

Well now, Father Bernard McGuire was going mad about this altogether and cursed the men who were building the hall. He swore that 'he would put horns on their heads!'

Now, a local character called Red Pat Jennings, 'The Pig Killer' (whom Kavanagh mentioned attending a wake with in his book *The Green Fool*), was known to have a gift for foreseeing a death before it happened. He said he could tell to the minute when the dying would become the dead. He travelled around the place castrating and dehorning animals. When he heard that the priest was going to put horns on the boys, he called by one day and said, 'Build away boys, I'll skull yez for nathin'.'

So the lads built away and Mullagh Hall was officially opened on New Year's Eve, 1940, with a dance!

Sadly the old hall has been closed for many years now and has lost its sparkle, but when I heard its story, like Kavanagh's poetry, its memory and magnitude were brought to life again.

As we headed back to the village of Inniskeen, I was pointed to the house of the local mill owner, where Patrick Pearse (commander-in-chief of the 1916 Easter Rising) had stayed one night in 1915 on his way to Carrickmacross.

Back in the centre of the village, we found ourselves outside Dan McNello's Bar. The red painted exterior and stone walls reminded me of Billy Brennan's barn. This was probably the place where Kavanagh got most of his courage to attend the dances at the barn.

Amazingly enough, Kavanagh was never barred from McNello's bar and he frequented it often during his lifetime when he was back in Inniskeen. I went inside and was given a warm welcome. I asked if I could take a look around. There was no issue with this and the artworks and photographs that captured some of the moments from the great poet's life were pointed out to me.

As I mentioned earlier that Kavanagh had never been barred from the pub, but unsurprisingly there were a couple of barmen that he did not get on with. There was one particular man – we won't mention his name – who was understood to be one of the best barmen in the country. Now, this man was not a great fan of Kavanagh and the feeling was mutual. Kavanagh was notorious for not having the money at hand for drink and some of the publicans would let him build up a tab, but this man would not – 'no money, no drink' was his policy.

Well, one day a local man named Ted McArdle and his son Peter were in the pub having a drink with Kavanagh. Ted McArdle was paying for the drink, as he usually did, for Kavanagh rarely had any money.

Ted and Kavanagh had a close friendship and Ted would have taken care of Kavanagh by getting him about and helping him out with a few pound every once in a while, and they enjoyed a drink together.

Well, there they were, having a drink, when who comes in. Only the new priest Father McCabe, looking to have a word with Kavanagh. So the priest asks Kavanagh what he would like to drink and he replies, 'I would like a gentleman's drink.' Now, for anyone who does not know what that is, it is a pint of porter (usually Guinness) and a full whiskey or a double (as opposed to a half or single). The barman in question had not heard of this before and could not serve him what he had asked for, so Kavanagh took the opportunity to have a go at him and point out how little he knew of his trade – he lambasted him something shocking. After that, he would never speak of Kavanagh again and those who knew him never asked.

It was only after Kavanagh died in 1967 that the local people of Inniskeen really realised the impact he'd had on the world.

Finally, I spoke to a local man from Inniskeen called Patsy Boylan, an earthy, straight-talking Monaghan man, who has a fairy field and fairy fort on his land.

He remembered Kavanagh as an odd sort of a man, who stuck out in the local community, wandering about the place talking to himself and wearing open-toed sandals with no socks. He said that Kavanagh was seen very much in the same light as another local eccentric called Packie Duffy, who was a communist and drove an Allgaier tractor, which was very unusual in Ireland.

Duffy would listen to Radio Moscow and never had any interest in the Church and never went to Mass, but he would always go to funerals.

I was to find out that this was the same Packie Duffy who put up the money for the building of Mullagh Hall.

He and Patsy Boylan had been to Kavanagh's funeral in the village and Patsy has never seen anything like it since. He said there were hundreds of people at it, from all over the country and further afield. He explained that many of the people who did not think too much of Kavanagh in Inniskeen and saw him just as a drunk with a bad attitude changed their tune after his funeral. They realised there was a lot more to him than met the eye.

I was also told that after he died, some of the locals who would have nothing to do with Kavanagh when he was alive had converted to adoring fans, for they wanted to be associated with his celebrity.

But there was definitely a softer and gentler side to Kavanagh and he certainly was ahead of his time in many ways. I was told that shortly before he died, Kavanagh was performing a reading from his work at the Poetry Centennial '67 in the Barbican, London, in the summer of 1967.

It was 'the summer of love' and Scott McKenzie was telling everyone to wear flowers in their hair if they were planning on going to San Francisco. In the midst of all this, auld Paddy Kavanagh was reciting his poetry to a young audience of hippies in London. His health was not great at all and he faltered at one point in his recital. He was embarrassed and thought that maybe he could not go on. Then out of the audience came some of these young hippies who stood on the stage beside him and threw flower petals at him. This gesture of kindness and compassion gave him the strength to go on and finish his piece. Kavanagh was so touched by what they had done for him that he composed these words celebrating the new and colourful world that was emerging around him:

But since the arrival of
The Beatles and Stones
Anything goes
And I am glad
That Freedom is mad
Dancing with pot
Hurray! Hurray!
I say
For this beautiful day ...

> Extempore at Poetry Centennial '67
> London, 14 July 1967

Patrick Kavanagh died on 30 November 1967, leaving behind him a collection of timeless and powerful works that will live on forever.

2

CASTLE LESLIE

*While travelling around Co. Monaghan and meeting various people
collecting folklore and stories, I was always asked if I had visited Castle
Leslie in Glaslough.*

*I had known of its existence but I knew very little about it, so I
took it upon myself to make contact with the people there and they
very kindly invited me over to the castle, where I was shown archival
material and predominantly the work of Sir John Randolph Leslie,
3rd Baronet (24 September 1885–14 August 1971), better known as
Shane Leslie.*

*The baronet was one of Ireland's great collectors of ghost stories and
a man whose diligent and in-depth research into strange phenomena
has given his writing real value. He also wrote poetry and prose and,
while he was at Cambridge University, changed his religion to Roman
Catholicism and was a great supporter of Irish Home Rule and the
Gaelic Revival. It was at this time also that he changed his name to
'Shane', an anglicised Irish version of his own name.*

*I was delighted to be given the go-ahead to reproduce some of Shane
Leslie's work by his grandson Mr Tarka King, the current holder of
Shane's copyright.*

*So it is with great pleasure that I share with you some of the work of
this fascinating and extraordinary man, along with some chilling ghost
stories from the magnificent Castle Leslie.*

When myself and my partner Paula Flynn went to Castle Leslie,
we met briefly with Sammy Leslie, Shane Leslie's granddaughter.
After these introductions, we were shown around the castle by

Yvonne. It is a magnificent building, with a vast estate, and it was a real privilege to be shown around its luxurious interior. We felt like we were on the set of an old film and the grand Victorian Gothic design of the old house had me looking out for Vincent Price, Peter Cushing and Christopher Lee, who might well have been lurking in the shadows.

Indeed, Castle Leslie is as atmospheric as it is impressive. The walls are bedecked with original artworks (I noticed a striking portrait of Shane Leslie by R.G. Eves painted in 1932) and each room has its own character and unique style. It was like we were being taken on a journey through time, design and culture.

As we were shown around the house, a room was pointed out, which was considered to be haunted. This room belonged to Norman Leslie, Shane's brother who died during the First World War. The bed in the room belonged to Shane's Aunt Clara (Mrs Morton Frewen). It originally came from a house in East Sussex called Brede Place, near the town of Battle, where the Battle of Hastings took place in 1066. The house was built in 1350 by one of Edward III's knights and it was rented in 1899 to the writer Stephen Crane. Aunt Clara had the house restored and when Shane's two sons Jack and Desmond, along with their sister Anita, were children, they used to stay at the house, but they were absolutely terrified of the place.

After old Aunt Clara died, the bed was moved to Castle Leslie and whatever phantom possessed the bed seemed to come with it. Some people who slept in the bed claimed that the bed levitated and other folk claimed that when they lay on the bed they felt something pressing down upon them. Others said that the bedroom door opened and banged shut all through the night. That said, the grandson of Guglielmo Marconi, the inventor of the wireless, stayed there and claimed that he never had such a peaceful night's sleep.

Now, there is a possibility that the reason for the bed's strange phenomena is the fact that its owner, Sir Goddard Oxenbridge (c. 1478–10 Feb. 1531), had a very dark secret. He was a well-respected member of society at the time and was chosen to be Sheriff of Surrey and Sussex three times. On 23 June 1509, to honour the coronation of Henry VIII and Katherine of Aragon, he was knighted. So, all in all, he seemed like a pretty upstanding chap. But he became known to the locals as 'The Brede Giant' or 'The Ogre of Oxenbridge' for he was a very large and well-built man with an imposing stature. Rumours about him were created by the country folk, which was a common practice at the time, when the peasantry were fearful of the gentry. It was said that he could not be harmed by metal weapons and that only wooden ones could kill him. It was also said that he ate a child every night for his supper and this was supported by the fact that several children had disappeared in the area at the time.

Well, the local children had had enough of old Oxenbridge, so they lured him to a bridge called Groaning Bridge at Stubb's Lane, where they got him drunk and then proceeded to saw his body in two with a wooden saw. Some people say that these stories were created by smugglers who used Brede Place to hide their stash and were known to create horror stories to scare folk away from their hiding places.

What I find fascinating about this story is its similarity to the story of 'Bluebeard', a 1697 fairy tale written by the great French storyteller Charles Perrault (author of 'Cinderella'). That story is based on Gilles de Rais (*c.* September 1405–26 October 1440). Gilles de Rais was Marshal of France and in 1429 he fought alongside Saint Joan of Arc. This was another guy with a very respectable-looking CV. But it also came to light that he too was a child-killer, which was the least of his crimes for he was a true and terrible monster in every sense. At last, justice was served and he was executed by hanging and burning on Wednesday, 26 October 1440.

Shane Leslie wrote a poem entitled 'Bluebeard', which I have included here. It is a dark and damning poem and certainly captures the insidious nature of its title character. I wonder if the connection with 'Brede Place', the haunted bed and Sir Goddard Oxenbridge inspired the menacing poem.

Sir Jack Leslie claimed to hear screams and groans coming from the room where the bed was kept and one night he saw a figure go up the stairs near the room. He assumed that this person was going to bed as people stayed at Castle Leslie on a regular basis. Sir Jack bid the stranger goodnight but they proceeded to go up the stairs to the attic, where all the old furniture was stored, and the figure simply disappeared.

Now, this room was, and still is, known as Norman's room. Norman was Shane Leslie's younger brother who was killed in October 1914, whilst charging a German machine gun armed with only a sword, which had been presented to him by HRH Prince Arthur, Duke of Connaught. The prince was a great friend of the family and visited the Castle Leslie estate on a regular basis in the early 1900s.

Norman appeared on the terrace of Castle Leslie a week before his death. The family were delighted that he had returned home safely from the terrible war. It was also reported that Norman had been seen walking around Glaslough, enjoying his favourite places of interest.

But things took a turn when he failed to show up at the castle for evening dinner and there was great concern as to his whereabouts. Not long after this, a telegram arrived, reporting his death at the Battle of Armentières. Norman's sword was lost during the battle until a Belgian farmer discovered it in the 1930s. It was traced back to its original owner and brought back to Glaslough. The sword is still used on ceremonial occasions at Castle Leslie.

After we heard these stories of the castle, we were taken to the archive, which was filled with old documents and books. It was here that I was introduced to the poetry of Shane Leslie. I was fascinated by the various subjects that he covered in his writing, from ghost stories to politics. There were five of his poems that I chose to reproduce in the book. They capture Shane Leslie's love of Monaghan and its folklore. He was fascinated by the fairy folk – or the Good Folk, as they are often referred to – and it is a subject that is very close to my own heart. I was both delighted and overwhelmed with all the fairy stories that I collected from Monaghan and have included in this book. These poems by Shane Leslie are wonderful and capture the imagination, taking you to fairyland, the dark world of Bluebeard and Co. Monaghan.

THE FAIRIES OF EM

So, without further ado, I present to you: 'Ballad of County Monaghan', 'Monaghan', 'Fairy Ballad', 'The Fairies of Emy' and 'Bluebeard' by Shane Leslie.

Ballad of County Monaghan

In Summer climes or Winter Times
Where'er I roam this lonesome world
Where'er my tent may be unfurled
I hist me murmur in a simple lay –
Oh give me Monaghan on a soft wet day!

Mid Arctic Gales and frozen Whales
When all the Ocean freezeth foam,
I curse the day I turned to roam
And could cry out loud into the spitting spray –
Just give me Monaghan on a soft wet day!

Mid torrid sands in Afric's lands
Remembering bogs of pliant green
And hedges thick with sapling treen
I hear my sinking heart turn round and say –
Oh give me Monaghan on a soft wet day!

When I have passed this world at last
And find that I am drawing nigh
A place that feels a little dry
Maybe that I will turn to God and pray –
Just give me Monaghan on a soft wet day!

Monaghan

MONAGHAN, mother of a thousand
Little moulded hills,
Set about with little rivers
Chained to little mills.

Rich and many-pastured Monaghan,
Mild thy meadows lie,
Melting to the distant mountains
On the mirrored sky.

Lovely, lowly-lying Monaghan
Oh thy little lakes
Float and tremble lordy lilies
Hoed by fairies' rakes.

Silvered o'er with sunshine, or by
Night and shimmering fog,
Where thy sloping cornland meets
Beauteous fields of bog.

Humbly hid with heath and lichen
Waits thy turf of old,
While thy hasty bees come hiding
Honey thro' thy mould.

Thro' and thro' thy restless rushes
Run a thousand rills,
Lisping long-forgotten little
Songs of Ireland's ills.

For thy mingled chaplet, oak and
Beechwood thou dost bind
Green in summer, and in the winter
Musical with wind.

Fairy Ballad

Where did you dream that snowy dress,
Oh fairy maid, with golden bars?

I snatched it from an Angel's loveliness
And left him naked in the stars

And how did you pick that pearly chain,
Oh fairy maid, around your neck?

I made my lovers weep and weep again
A thousand tears to make each speck.

And why did you get those ruby shoon,
O fairy maid, to trip the mud?

I stole them from the baby in the Moon,
To dip them, dearest, in your blood!

The Fairies of Emy

The Fairies of Emy were out on the fort,
Just once in the year is their right,
For music and dancing and sport
The half of a mad summer's night.
Old tunes they were playing, old measures they brought,
And hushed them again before light.

The scolags and farmers they spoiled of their silk
And heaped all the bran on the floor:
They left all the salt in the ale,
The butter they slid through the door:
Then laughing they lapped up the milk,
And shouted in Irish for more.

The priest's foreign hen's got no sleep in the night
With fairies that climbed on the sill,
And hammered and battered the eggs for a bite
To give their wee bodies a fill:
They climbed in the shells, and God save us the sight,
They sailed round the pool of the mill.

A poor little child at the foot of the glen
Lay dead and unsigned of the cross:
They kissed him and carried him out of the ken
Of parents who wept of his loss:
They gave him the shoon of the fairy men
And set him to dance on the moss.

Bluebeard

He still could hear the embers from his sleep,
Creak through the night to long and late;
Till all the dust of day was gathered deep
On cloth and goblet and on plate.

From chapel floor his first beloved rose up;
'Is yon dish sweeter than any I gave?'
The second cried, 'Doth fairer hand fill up your cup?'
But the third, 'I keep thy sheet in my grave'.

His first love hissed, 'Ere dawn your marrow and sap
Shall be made to meet for the eaters in red.'
The second, 'A white-eyed slug to your heart shall lap.'
The third, 'I shall bind up the wounds of thee dead.'

His first love said, 'By your pain be I fatted and filled!'
The second cried, 'I will drink of your hell!'
And the third one said; whom to he had wedded and killed;
'Alas, and alas! But I love thee well.'

He never heard the ashes in his sleep
Stir dying till the sun rose late;
For all the dust of the night gathered deep
On cloth and goblet and on plate.

3

THE GHOST TRAIN

I found the bones of this haunting tale in a wee book called Irish
Ghosts *(2002) by J. Aeneas Corcoran. The version I found was very
short but I have heard so much about the old defunct train lines in
Monaghan that I decided to make it a bit more elaborate and give it
the attention that it deserved.*

Hear that phantom whistle blow ... All aboard!

It was the summer of 1924, and two men were waiting on a train
from Clones to Armagh. That line is gone now and no trains have
run on it since 1957. But in the summer of 1924, the trains were
up and running and there were plenty of folk happy to use the
service.

Well, it was a quiet evening at Clones railway station in Co.
Monaghan and the two men sat on a bench outside the waiting
room. Both of them had passed through the waiting room and
noticed that there was no one there. It was such it a lovely evening
that they decided that it would make a lot more sense to wait
outside.

As they sat there, they could hear a low moaning sound coming
from the waiting room behind them. They were sure they could
hear a man's voice calling out for help. Well, they got up from
the bench and had a look inside the waiting room, but there was
nothing there apart from two long benches and the long narrow
table placed between them.

This was very strange indeed. They went back to sitting outside
again. As they did, they could hear a train coming. At this stage,

they were both quite relieved to hear their train coming as they had been quite spooked by the sounds coming from the eerie waiting room. The noise of the approaching train grew louder and they could hear the whistle blow, but they could see no smoke in the distance. The sound of the train grew louder and louder. They jumped to their feet for it was as if the train was almost upon them. They felt a ferocious breeze as the train rushed passed them. One of the men had his cap blown off by the force of the breeze. They stood there bemused, for there was no train, and as the phantom locomotive whizzed passed them, they heard a terrible scream coming from the waiting room behind them.

The poor men were terrified. They were frozen to the spot. As the sound of the invisible train began to fade, the terrible cries and moans behind them began to subside. When all was silent again, the men saw the signalman come out of his office, looking for the train that he had heard but not seen. The men were relieved that at least they were not losing their minds as the signalman had experienced the same thing they had. They told him that they had heard, felt and even smelt the train as it passed by them. And they told him about the terrible sounds they heard coming from the waiting room.

The signalman stared at both of them with a strange look in his eye. He took a deep breath and told them that some poor man had jumped in front of a train from the station the year previous. His mangled body had been brought into the waiting room, where he died an agonising death on that narrow long table that stands between the two benches.

4

THE TALE OF CRICKET McKENNA

This is a great wee Monaghan story that was passed on to me by my friend and fellow storyteller, Francis McCarron.

Once there was a man called Patrick McKenna who lived in the parish of Errigal Truagh in north County Monaghan. But if you went to find him, you would have your work cut out for you because there are lots and lots of McKennas in north Monaghan. As a matter of fact, there are so many McKennas that they all have nicknames. There are the Barneys, the Big Frankies, the Deleavys, the Hughies, the Myleses, the Pat Arts, the Red Oineys, the Roes, the Rosses, the Toals, the Yellow Willies and many more.

But the man in our story was called Cricket McKenna. This might have been because he had spindly legs like a cricket or it may have been because he was light on his feet or it may even have been because his mind hopped about like a cricket's. Whatever the reason, Cricket was the name he was given and it stuck.

He was the sort of a man that would chance his luck at anything, even things he knew nothing about. His mother often warned him that, 'Long runs the fox, but he's caught at last!', but that never sank in with Cricket.

During the famine, things were very hard for the people in Cricket's part of the country, so he decided to leave home in search of work to earn money to buy food or even to work for food as wages so he wouldn't starve.

As he walked the road from Truagh, he passed through the village of Tydavnet on his way towards Monaghan town. All along the roadside, the crickets sang in the hedges. But if the crickets were plentiful, food was scarce and he was soon ready to drop with the hunger. He came to the townland of Cornacassa, where a local landlord, D'Acre Hamilton, had his estate. A sign at the entrance read, 'Trespassers will be hanged'.

Oh well, thought Cricket, if I'm going to die, it might as well be while trying to live, and so he went up the avenue to Hamilton's big house to see if he could get some food. He hadn't got very far when the owner himself came roaring up towards him.

'Where do you think you're going?' he bellowed. 'Can you not read? I'll have no trespassers on my land.'

'I'm no trespasser,' said Cricket, 'just an honest man in search of work.'

'What work can you do?' enquired Hamilton.

'I'm a spayman. I can see things, I can know things, I can find things out and say how they are.'

'Indeed,' said the landlord. 'Well, an emerald ring has gone missing in this house. If you can say where it is, you will be given a bag of gold coins, but if you can't, I'll have you hanged for the trespasser you are!'

'Finding a ring is a difficult piece of work,' said Cricket. 'It will take me three days and during those three days I must be given my food and lodgings and then I will be able to get the ring.'

'See to it that you do,' warned Hamilton. He bellowed for a servant to show Cricket to a room.

Now, there were three serving girls in the house and they had stolen the ring. When they heard of Cricket's arrival, they discussed their situation. On the first morning of his stay, the eldest girl brought him breakfast. Cricket blessed himself and said out loud, 'Glory be to the Father and to the Son and to the Holy Ghost,' and then he was silent as he ate the food. At least I have two more breakfasts before I die, he thought, as he had no idea how he would find the ring.

The eldest girl returned to her two companions.

'He is bluffing,' she said. 'He hasn't got a clue.'

On the next day, the second girl brought him his breakfast. Cricket blessed himself and said out loud, 'Glory be to the Father and to the Son and to the Holy Ghost,' and then he was silent as he ate the food. A day left, he thought, and I'm no further forward.

The second girl returned to her two companions.

'We are as safe as houses,' she said. 'He is no more a spayman than I am.'

On the third morning, the youngest girl brought him breakfast. She was much more nervous and afraid than the other two. Cricket blessed himself and said out loud, 'Glory be to the Father and to the Son and to the Holy Ghost,' and then he was silent as he ate the food. I know I am going to hang today, he thought, but at least I'll not die of the hunger.

'Do you know?' asked the young girl.

'Oh,' said Cricket, thinking she meant the fate in store for him, 'I know all indeed.'

At these words, the young girl began to cry.

'Oh please don't tell we took the ring,' she wailed, 'or we'll all be hanged.'

'Give me the ring and tell me what happened,' said the quick-thinking Cricket, 'and everything will be all right.'

The girls told all and gave Cricket the ring. He wrapped it in a potato skin and threw it out into the yard, where a flock of ducks were standing. It landed in front of a green drake that was wad-dling by. The drake gobbled the skin up and waddled on.

Cricket's heart soared like a bird and he wandered out into the yard whistling a tune. Before long, D'Acre Hamilton came charg-ing up.

'Well,' he roared, 'you've had your three days. Where is my emerald ring and what happened to it?'

'That's easily told,' said Cricket. 'The ring got thrown out by accident with the potato skins.' He pointed to the green drake in the middle of the flock of ducks. 'Right now, it's inside that large green drake.'

'Not a word about it,' roared Hamilton, with disbelief written all over his large face.

He ordered a farmhand to kill the drake. But when the farm-hand did and they looked inside, there was the ring.

Well, D'Acre Hamilton could not get over it. He thought Cricket was the greatest man alive and did not want to let him leave his service. But Cricket was anxious to get away and requested his payment. Hamilton gave him his bag of gold, but begged him to stay until he could at least show him to the other landlords. He sent word for them to come at once and meet the great spayman and he told them of his powers.

Cricket shared some of his good fortune with the serving girls and was preparing to leave as the neighbouring landlords arrived. Rossmore, Lesley and Woodwright looked Cricket up and down and listened to D'Acre Hamilton's tale with wonder and some incredulity. Now, as I said before, crickets were very plentiful that year and one was singing in the hedge beside Mr Woodwright. The landlord reached out and caught it in his fist and held his closed hand out towards Cricket McKenna. 'If you are such a good man at your job,' he said, 'I will give you the same again in gold as Mr Hamilton if you can tell me what I am holding in my hand.'

Poor Cricket hadn't a notion. He knew the game was up. He turned to Woodwright and said, 'My mother was right in what she used to say, "Long runs poor cricket, but he is caught at last!"'

He was right again! And with Hamilton's gold and Woodwright's gold safely in his pocket, he lived as happy as any man with gold can live until the day he died.

5

THE BALLAD OF SEAN BEARNA (SHANE BEARNACH)

This is a piece I found in the Tydavnet Journal *of 1995. Its author is unknown but it is a fascinating piece and tells the tale of the legendary highwayman Sean Bearna.*

The rising moon was wading round the shoulder of the hill
And the heath bell bent before the breeze to kiss the mountain rill;
A white mist veiled the rushy glen and fringed the dark lough shore
With trailing wisps around the base of lofty Carnmore.

No reaper's song among the sheaves nor happy laugh is heard
No shouting school boy in the lane no lilt of homing bird
For bright and clear the lights appear on yonder darkened scar
And the robber Saxon trembles in the lowland plains afar.

What the beacon fires that limn the dark and light the mountain side,
What sign to blanch the Saxon wolves that in the vales abide,
You lurid banner of the night from moor and lonesome glen
To hasty meeting place calls forth Sean Bearna and his men.

Ay' well may yonder cravens crouch and well may fear the blade,
They drove the hapless peasant from the sheltered lowland glade

And condemned him on the rock and heath and floe of Wild Slieve
    Beagh
To skull and starve while down below the bodach lord holds sway.

And now the moon is clear at last, the veiling clouds are fled,
But thicker hangs the shrouding mist like winding sheet of dead;
A startled grouse resounds the night a dreaming curlew calls
And soft as lowing herd at eve, the flow of Cuskers falls.

But fling the faggot to the flame, bear out the brand anew,
Unfurl the flag of fire and paint the sky a bloody hue,
For yonder from this deep recess, the border king is come
To wreak revenge upon the spawn that drove us from our home.

Sean Bearna rode within the light his steed a dappled grey;
His tail and mane were streaming like the first pale shoots of day;
Nor cleaner limb nor fleeter ever fought the surging flood
Or left the foeman far behind in deep Drumfurrer wood

While Sean, as straight as mountain ash as tall as mountaineer,
His curling jet black hair hangs down to shade his bandoleer,
A broad sword and a musket were the only arms he knew,
As marshalled he his men the robber Saxon to subdue.

'To horse!' the swift command is e'en more speedily obeyed
And three score fleet curvetting steeds are mounted for the raid
And three score gallant rapparees with ready hand on rein
Repress the prancing steeds as bold Sean Bearna speaks again.

'They drove us from our happy homes, a price upon our heads,
The changing sky to be our roof and the heather for our bed;
Bold outlawed men we only wait for vengeance swift and sure
But then we'll take the grabbers wealth and give it to the poor.'

He swings the dappled charger round, he draws the naked steel;
One flaming flourish in the moon, one stroke of armoured hail,
Then swift as mountain flood they ride by ford and rushy glen
To seek revenge on those who wronged Sean Berna and his men.

The sleeping peasant hearkens that wild drumming on the night
And through frosted pane beholds like shadow in the light
As speeding troop across the hill then silent as before,
Save where the startled watch dog lifts a cry beside the door.

And speeding still the border land is far upon the road,
With flag of flame unfurled again and fanned in Ballinode.
'God save ye, Wright and Mitchell, ere this bloody night is o'er,
We'll raze your feudal piles and make a fire of Mullaghmore.'

'Pass round the herd, lead out the steeds, no time for delay;
On Eshnagloch we'll bed then at the dawning of the day,
Let scarlet soldier follow on with pitch cap, lash and blade,
Sean Bearna and his trusty men will meet him unafraid.'

'Tis morning on the grey hills' crest, gold splashed the eastern sky,
The meadows bathing in the dew with sailing clouds on high,
His song the waking moor-hen holds the crouches in the grass
As troopers' steed and tyrant blade in swift procession passed.

They rein the mettled charges ere the mountain they begin,
Then reckless ride the steep ascent of health bound Eshacrin,
But safe within the gloomy caves of lone Meenamen Glen
On couch of sedge and heather rest Sean Berna and his men.

Thrice forty summer suns have bathed shoulder of the hill
Yet round the hearth-fire's blaze the outlaw's name is sounded still
And the hunter marking out the chase will stiffen in his chair
To tell of speeding Black and Tan behind Sean Bearna's lair.

But saddest tale of all, the death that claimed the border king
'Twas Saxon gold that loosed the shaft and stilled the wild hawk's
    wing
And lonely shepherds on the round still meet in moor and glen
When hangs the moon a ghastly troop Sean Bearna and his men.

Sean Bearna rode within the light, his steed a dappled grey,
His tail and mane were streaming like the first pale shades of day

Nor cleaner limb nor fleeter, ever fought the surging flood
Or left the foeman far behind, in deep Drumfurrer wood.

On one such night, Sean Bearna went on a predatory excursion to the Gola estate. Attended by his hard-riding mountainy men, he circled the lawn and the estate, herding the sheep, the cattle, the horses and swollen droves and heading for the mountain. Before leaving, the fire brand was laid to the straw pile, the blazing pine showing the wooden structure. Flames soared into the teeth of the wind. As burning timbers crashed to the ground around the robber band, a company of redcoats came from a column. Dismay reigned and there was a confusion of stampeding and fighting in the ranks of the rapparees. The dappled grey was wounded, his stride was shortened. Through the black water stream and into the breast of the dear dark mountain trailed the outlaws, with the grey taking up the rear.

On Strawmacelroy, Sean Bearna was drowned. He shot his dappled charger and turned to face his foes. On Strawmacelroy was taken Sean Bearna and when morning paled in the east his body lay mutilated on the hill. His head was raised high on a spear in the resting camp of the enemy. To the town rode his majesty's militia, with the head of the rapparee tied up in a bag.

But saddest tale of all, in death
Was claimed the border king
'Twas Saxon gold that loosed the
  shaft
And stilled the wild hawk's
  wing.

Behind Meenamar Hill are the stables of Sean Bearna and the little lake nearby. Once, on a day when the redcoats were closing on him, Sean Bearna swam that little lake and when he dived into the dark waters, he found an entrance, one of many, to his retreat. Tradition has it that his great wealth is on the muddied floor of the lake. One day, a mountainy man with greed in his heart went forth to seek the treasure trove, but he was never seen again. Fairy music emanates from the sturdy rock pile of the long-dead rapparee and the fairy lights twinkle about the stables. On bright nights when the moon is up, the figure of the Slieve Beagh King appears erect and defiant, his feet in the blossomed tendrils of the heather.

6

GILDER – A TRUE CHARACTER

This is the story of Gilder, a wise man of Monaghan who had a cure for many ailments.

We speak a lot about old characters when we talk about the past. These are people who stand out and have certain quirks that set them apart from others. On this journey, I have come across my fair share of characters, but when I get my 'story shovel' out and dig up the past, those days when television and radio weren't even an option, never mind a luxury, it's there that I find the real authentic characters – the ones who were not being 'quirky' for any reason other than that was just how they were made. They were cut that way.

'Gilder' was the definition of a character. He was called James Agnew, but people in the locality called him various names, including 'Gildernew' and 'Gilder Agnew', but most of the time he just got plain old 'Gilder'.

Gilder was known to have special powers. I suppose he would've been a wise man or witch doctor of the time. He was believed to have cures for certain ailments, including ringworm and skin conditions. Some say he was able to cure both man and beast and he was known for working well with horses, in particular.

He lived in a little cabin with his sister Ketty, in a place called Toneystaken in Co. Monaghan. This may seem idyllic and some of us might visualise a wooden house with a front porch and a bright red door and flowers on the windowsills. But sadly that wasn't the reality for Gilder and Ketty. For they couldn't have lived any further away from comfort. One person described the house in this way: 'A hole in the roof served as a chimney, doors nor windows they had none, just a bag nailed over an opening in the wall for a door.' So when someone travelled to see Gilder, they may well have been dubious of his skills.

From talking to people, it seems that Gilder had no fear and had little or no respect for the clergy or authority figures of any kind. He relied on his funny wee ways and his sense of humour to get by and, in many cases, to get him out of tricky situations.

The land that Gilder and Ketty's home was on was owned by a land agent and the man in charge was James Rodgers. There was a set day for paying the rent and so the people would queue up and wait their turn to pay. One day, when Gilder's turn came, he approached Mr Rodgers with a smile and said, 'Hello Jimmy.'

Mr Rodgers said, 'Have you got my rent?'

'No, I haven't,' Gilder replied.

'Well, why not?'

So Gilder said back to him, 'Ah, you're in bad form today, Mr Rogers. I'll come back some other day when you're in better form.' And off he went.

This kind of interaction reminds me of Francie Brady from *The Butcher Boy*. Like Francie's character, Gilder seems to have been untouchable. Although we don't know the full story and we have no idea of the aftermath and the consequences he faced. From the recollections and the stories that have been passed down, he seems to have been a law unto himself. He feared nobody.

Gilder was a rough sort of a man – a raw man, as they would say in the country. He said what was on his mind. Maybe he was brought up that way and knew no better. In 1832, his father was sentenced to death for forging a £1 note, but later the charge was dropped.

What really upset Gilder the most was the death of his mother. When she died, the parish priest tried to console him by telling him that his mother was happy now in heaven. So when it came to the month's mind, the priest returned to Gilder's house to make arrangements for the Mass but Gilder said to him, 'You told me she was already in heaven, so if she is then why would I want her to be any higher!' He then walked away, leaving the priest to make of that what he wanted.

Was he trying to save a few pound by not having a Mass? Was he being funny? Or did he actually believe what the priest had told him?

Another story involving a priest was the story of the priest who brought a pony to Gilder for a cure (I'm not sure if it was the same priest). The pony had a bad skin condition and he thought Gilder would be the right man for the job. Gilder took a good look at the pony, sighed a few times, threw his eyes up towards heaven a few times and maybe even down towards hell. Every so often, he would take a look at the priest and then focus on the horse again. He just keep circling the horse in silence until he eventually stopped and stood in front of the animal and he asked the priest, 'Where did you get him?'

The priest said, 'I bought him at the fair.'

And Gilder replied (as serious and deadpan as can be), 'Well, you must have been blind or drunk that day.'

So he walked into his house and came back out with a bag of oats and who knows what else and fed it to the pony, and the condition was cleared up within a few days.

Another man travelled miles to see Gilder, all the way from Fivemiletown in Armagh, which is almost twenty miles away.

Apparently the man was well-to-do and was dressed in his finest pinstriped suit. So Gilder decided he would give him the cure, but first he got him to clean out his byre ('byre' is a fancy word for a cow barn). The man had no choice because only Gilder had what he wanted. Gilder had him right where he wanted him – knee deep in cow dung.

Gilder was no stranger to the law. At one point he had to make a visit to a solicitor. After the consultation, the solicitor asked him for a payment for his services and Gilder turned to him and said, 'For what?'

He said, 'For my advice.'

Gilder stood up and said, 'Ah, but I am not going to take your advice!' And off he went about his business.

Was Gilder as witty as Oscar Wilde or was he just a wild countryman?

It's hard to tell whether Gilder was just a simple man or whether he was taking everyone for a ride. It seems he took advantage of situations and had a laugh to himself when people's backs were turned. Gilder was meant to have looked much older than he was and the only photograph I could find suggests he was an old, old man and could pass for 90 or more ... but in actual fact he died young, at only 64 ... and I have no idea when the picture was taken. But one thing is for sure: Gilder was a true character who is still being talked about almost 100 years later.

7

THE WILDE SISTERS

This is a well-known story from Co. Monaghan about the tragic lives of Oscar Wilde's two half-sisters.

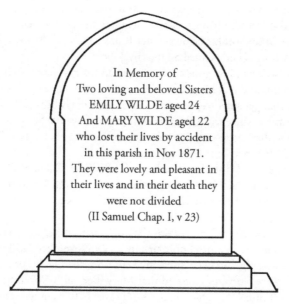

In Memory of
Two loving and beloved Sisters
EMILY WILDE aged 24
And MARY WILDE aged 22
who lost their lives by accident
in this parish in Nov 1871.
They were lovely and pleasant in
their lives and in their death they
were not divided
(II Samuel Chap. I, v 23)

This is the heartfelt inscription on the gravestone that was erected for the half-sisters of Oscar Wilde, who lost their young lives tragically in a fire in Co. Monaghan in 1871.

You can visit this grave, if you wish. Just a short distance south-west of Monaghan town, on the road to Clones, there is a signpost which reads 'Drumsnatt Church of Ireland'. To the rear of this small country church is the grave where the two sisters were laid to rest a long, long time ago.

The sisters in question, who lost their lives in a fire in a nearby manor house, were the half-sisters of the Irish poet, novelist and dramatist, Oscar Wilde, who was born in Dublin in 1854. Oscar was only 18 when his half-sisters died, but loss and heartache were already known to him. Five years before the tragic event, when Oscar was just 12, he had lost his younger sister Isola, who died at only 10 years of age, after a bout of fever, at the home of her aunt, Margaret Nobel, in Edgeworthstown, Co. Longford.

Isola's death had a traumatic effect on Oscar Wilde and he was said to have been inconsolable for months afterwards. When he died in 1900, his possessions included an envelope containing some strands of his beloved sister Isola's hair, with the inscription 'My Isola's Hair' penned on the envelope.

Oscar had just gone to Trinity when his two half-sisters died and it is said that his grief was not at all on the same scale as when his younger sister passed away. This is most likely because he knew them less since the girls were only his half-sisters. Some sources argue that Oscar may not have known them at all, because Emily and Mary may have been kept secret.

They shared the same father – Sir William Wilde of Dublin. Despite the fact, however, that their father attended their funeral, it is believed that he was terribly grief-stricken and heartsick, having to bury two more of his children.

The *Northern Standard* was the only paper in the area to report the tragedy, in a brief obituary in its 25 November 1871 issue. Their deaths had been discreetly kept from the Dublin press. The *Northern Standard* reported that Mary died on 8 November and that 'Emma', by which name Emily was better known, died on the 21 November. Normally something so tragic would have been more widely publicised, but it was obviously kept under wraps to preserve Sir William's reputation.

According to Julian Hanna (2015), in his essay 'Death by Fire: The Secret of the Wilde Sisters' in the online magazine *Numéro*

Cinq, the first published account of the story appeared in a biography of William Wilde by T.G. Wilson in 1942.

Emily and Mary Wilde were living in Co. Monaghan and were being looked after by a relative, a Rev. Ralph Wilde, rector of St Molua's, Drumsnat, who was the brother of their father.

The night of the fire was Halloween night. A party had been arranged to celebrate All Hallow's Eve, or *Samhain* in Ireland, and because the girls were popular with the local people, they were invited to a ball in a manor house called Drumaconnor House. The man who owned the house was Mr Andrew Reed, a local bank manager. This house still exists and is still known by the same name. Currently it serves as a B&B, just off the Monaghan–Clones road.

After the other guests had gone home, the two girls remained for a while longer and a gentleman took one of them for a final dance around the floor (it is said that the gentleman was Mr Andrew Reid, the host of the party), but as they glided past the open fireplace, her crinoline caught fire. Her sister ran to her rescue and in the hysteria her sister's dress also caught fire. Those in attendance tried to smother the flames by wrapping garments around both girls and some stories say that those who remained at the ball carried the girls out and rolled them in the snow.

Local historian Eamonn Mulligan, co-author of '*The Replay': A Parish History* (a history of the parish of Kilmore and Drumsnat, published in 1984), explained that in their efforts to conceal the whole tragic episode and to shield the person of Sir William from further adverse publicity, the family name of the Wilde sisters was actually altered to read 'Wylie' in several later reports, particularly in two reports written by the coroner for the county, Mr Alexander C. Waddell, who was clearly influenced by the stern request from Sir William Wilde that no inquest be held. Instead, an inquiry was held, to be followed by a second inquiry, but no inquest. Both of the coroner's reports are quoted in full by one of Co. Monaghan's leading historians, Mr Theo McMahon, in the 2003 edition of *Clogher Record*, of which Theo was editor of several years. The second of the two reports is somewhat similar in content to the first. It reads as follows:

On Wednesday 22nd November 1871 the death of Miss M Wylie, daughter of Sir William Wylie, was reported to me as resulting from very serious injuries caused by her clothes accidentally catching fire from those of her sister Miss L Wylie on the night of 31st October in the house of Mr Reed of Drumaconnor. In accordance with the report I attended the residence of Mr Reed where she had been an invalid since the painful occurrence. From all the circumstances of the case, same as those attendant on the death of her sister, I did not consider anything further necessary than a careful inquiry into the facts, which showed that everything possible was done to preserve the life of the deceased.

Crinoline dresses were fashionable during that period and they caused the deaths of many young women. It is easy to imagine how the tragedy occurred. So simple: in moments, the atmosphere would have changed and panic would have set in. It is also easy to understand why her sister ran to help. Her kindness and selflessness caused her to die also.

The crinoline is a woman's large petticoat that has come in and out of fashion since the early nineteenth century. The original garment was made from very stiff horsehair fabric that kept the fashionable hoop skirts of the 1800s in their proper position.

In 1864, the *New York Times* reported that almost 40,000 women throughout the world had died because of crinoline fires. I read about how dangerous crinoline was in an article on the *Vintage News* website (2016):

> As fashionable as the crinoline was, it became one of the most dangerous articles of clothing ever known. It was highly flammable, any women who witnessed the flames were unable to help for fear of their own skirts catching fire. It is reported that in Philadelphia, nine ballerinas were killed when one brushed by a candle at the Continental Theater.

The deaths of Emily and Mary are still very much spoken about among the people of Kilmore/Drumsnatt parish and the people are extremely grateful to Eamonn Mulligan and Father Brian McCluskey, co-authors of *'The Replay'*, and to leading historian Theo McMahon for researching the subject in such depth as their work will help keep the story alive for future generations of folklorists and historians in north Monaghan and beyond.

Julian Hanna states that the aftermath of the tragedy was, if possible, even more gruesome than the terrible accident itself. He is of the opinion that to die on Halloween night would have been merciful: instead, the young women lingered on for days and weeks at Drumaconnor. He goes on to say that the sisters remained in the house, as was the custom at the time, where they were treated for the severe burns they had both suffered. Mary, the younger sister who had tried to help, died first, on 9 November. Her death was kept a secret from Emily, who was also near death, to spare her the shock; nevertheless, three weeks after the accident, on 21 November, Emily also died.

Hanna writes about the local legend of the 'woman in black' – thought to be the girls' mother – who visited the graves regularly for twenty years after the tragedy. I have heard this from several people in Monaghan. Oscar Wilde also used to tell the story of a woman in black. Wilde, who was still a teenager at the time, recalled an unknown woman's visits to his house during his father's last illness. The woman would come into the house and kneel by William's sickbed, while Oscar's mother stood by, watching without interfering, apparently aware that her husband and the woman, who shared a tragic bond, had loved each other deeply.

I heard from one source that the 'woman in black' would travel by train from Dublin to Monaghan and make her way to the girls' grave, say a prayer and return to Dublin. It is said that she wore a black veil and would not speak if approached by someone.

8

SMUGGLING STORIES

When I was travelling around Co. Monaghan, talking to all the different characters that I met along the way, in between their wonderful stories about ghosts, fairies and wild folk, I would always hear wee tales about smuggling.

Customs controls were introduced between the borders of Northern Ireland and the Republic shortly after the establishment of the Irish Free State on 1 April 1923, 'April Fool's Day'. In fact, when the customs checkpoints and the men in their wee uniforms were introduced, the locals believed that it was all part of an elaborate joke.

Sadly, this was not the case, but the people did often outsmart and outwit these customs men.

The controls were operational and at times quite severe, up until 1 January 1993, when systematic customs checks were done away with between European Community member states upon the establishment of the Single Market.

But with the new Brexit laws and the United Kingdom leaving the European Union, these hard borders and custom controls could come back.

And if they do, so too will the inevitable acts of smuggling and more stories will follow.

Monaghan is bordered by six counties, three of which are part of the United Kingdom. Those three are Tyrone, Fermanagh and Armagh and the other three, which are in the Republic, are Meath, Louth and Cavan.

As Monaghan is right in the middle of these six counties, it was a perfect location for smuggling goods from the north to the south and vice versa.

I was told many stories about smuggling and I would like to take this opportunity to share them with you as the stories have become local folklore of a sort. However, I will refrain from using any of the names of the characters in the stories for various reasons. But maybe you just might recognise a few of them yourself …

When I set out on my journey to gather stories in Co. Monaghan, my first point of contact was the library in Clones, where I had been invited to tell stories by Deirdriu McQuaid the previous year. I enquired about local characters who would be good to get in touch with. I was sent without hesitation to the house of Dan Kerr. I was told that he was a man of 96 years of age and had plenty of tales to tell.

When I arrived at his house in Clones, I was surprised to find that he looked a lot younger than his years. He was only too happy to tell me some of the stories he knew.

In between endless cups of tae and slices of homemade fruit cake, we talked about his time working on the buses and how, back in the 1950s, Patrick Kavanagh had been one of his regular customers.

As we talked, it felt like I was on one of Dan's old bus routes, with various people coming and going from his house, some delivering coal and hot dinners and some just dropping in to say hello.

He talked about well-known Monaghan characters, some of whom were known for being good, whilst others were renowned for less admirable activities, such as smuggling.

The first fella he told me about used to go over the border from Monaghan to Armagh on a regular basis with a bicycle. Now, the customs men were getting a bit suspicious of this boy, who kept coming and going over the border with a bike that he always cycled from Monaghan but walked with when returning from Armagh.

This went on for quite a while until they noticed, upon closer inspection, that the tyres of the bike were worn when he was leaving Monaghan but when he was coming back from Armagh, he had lovely new tyres on the bike, which looked like they had never been used.

Well, it turned out that this boy was smuggling tyres and doing very well out of it until he was rumbled by the customs men.

Now, there was another fella that Dan talked about, who wanted to bring back a turkey for his wife one Christmas back in the 1950s. Monaghan was short of turkeys at the time and they were more plentiful in the North. So off he went and he got himself a turkey and was happily bringing it back to his wife when he was stopped at the border by the customs man. He was quizzed about where he had got the fowl from and where he was taking it. Unfortunately, there was no getting around it. He had no alibi except that he was taking it back to his wife, and he knew that she would be very disappointed when he returned without the festive bird. (Northern Ireland (UK) was short of turkeys at the time and they were more plentiful in County Monaghan as it is in Republic of Ireland, and therefore not subject to post-wartime rationing.)

Well, the customs man took pity on the poor fella and it was Christmas after all, so he wrote him a note stating, 'Please allow this one Turkey to pass', or something like that, and he put a special stamp on it, just to make it all official.

Well now, Dan told me that this same man used this wee note at as many different border patrols as there were and in doing so smuggled scores of turkeys across the border!

So I bid my farewells to Dan Kerr and shook his hand, the same hand that had shaken the hand of Patrick Kavanagh all those years ago.

The next man I met was Danny Aughey in Monaghan town. We met at the Westenra Arms Hotel in the centre of Monaghan. Danny had some fantastic stories to tell about Monaghan, some he had heard and some from his own experience growing up in Glaslough.

One of the stories he told from his childhood involved a man smuggling tobacco.

It all happened when Danny and a few of his friends were travelling home from school by train from Monaghan back to Glaslough. They were all in a box car, which held around ten passengers. Being in a box car also meant that you had to stay in the

carriage and could not move to a different carriage whilst the train was moving.

Now, as they were waiting for the train to move off, the carriage door was opened by an auld farmer, who had decided to come down from Armagh to Monaghan to do a bit of smuggling.

He asked them where they were going and they answered 'Glaslough'. With that, the farmer replied, 'That'll do', and he proceeded to get into the carriage with them.

Now, in the late 1940s and during the 1950s, tobacco was scare in the North, so this fella had come to Monaghan and bought around ten plugs of tobacco and was taking them back over the border.

He asked the boys if they would take a plug each and hide them for him, as he didn't have enough room under his hat to hide all the tobacco.

Well, the lads agreed that they would each take a plug of tobacco. They put the tobacco into their school bags. As there were four of them in total, the farmer was able to put the other six plugs inside his hat. The customs did occasionally check school bags, but these boys were well known and Danny's father worked as a signalman at Glaslough Station, so they were all right.

Shortly afterwards, the customs man got on and looked at the boys and the auld fella in the carriage. He turned to the farmer and asked him if he had anything to declare. The farmer said that he did not and that he had just been at the fair and was on his way home. Well, the customs man must have smelt a rat because he asked the poor auld fella to stand up and the customs man proceeded to tap his coat pockets. He asked him to open the coat and then he checked his jacket. The customs man seemed happy enough with this and was about to turn around and get off the train when one of the young fellas (Danny never said who it was) got up and lifted the hat off the poor old farmer. Well, as you can imagine, the tobacco fell out from under his hat onto the floor of the carriage and the customs man lifted the tobacco and then lifted the auld farmer off the train too.

Now, as Danny said, these customs men were quite scary as they wore a uniform very similar to what a guard would wear, with the hat and the uniform and all the rest, so the poor auld farmer was pretty worried by all of this. He was taken to the office, where he would have been fined and would have had his contraband confiscated. A while later, the boys saw him coming out of the office again, looking pretty shook up. He got onto a different box car a bit further up.

Well, the lads felt very guilty about their wee prank and thought it would be a good idea to give the four remaining pouches to the old man. But they could not do it at the station as they would be caught and they could not get to him through the other carriages, so they had to wait until they got off at Glaslough. When they did, they ran over to the old man's carriage and handed him his remaining plugs of tobacco, apologising for their mean trick.

Now, as Danny had mentioned before, his father worked as a signalman at Glaslough Station, and his father had told him the story of Sam's Bridge, which is just outside Monaghan town and was part of the old railway line from Glaslough to Monaghan. There is now a filling station named after it outside of Monaghan town.

This is one of the more sinister stories that I heard about the smuggling business. According to Danny's father, the events took place around the turn of the last century. During this period, pigs were slaughtered at home, as opposed to in slaughterhouses, and then they were salted and put in large jute sack, which is a large sack with a piece of rope sewn into the hem that can be closed and tightened by pulling on the rope.

These sacks were placed into a carriage at Glaslough and then were sent off to Belfast to a dealer. Now, there were always three or four pigs short on the Glaslough train and no one could understand how this was happening.

Well, it turned out that this fellow called Sam Bán (meaning 'White Sam') was sneaking onto the carriage before they loaded it and hiding in one of its dark corners with some old sacks pulled over himself. Now, this type of carriage would have been called a freight wagon and it would have had falling sides and an open top. This came in handy for Sam because, when the train would leave Glaslough, there was a steep hill shortly afterwards and the train could not build up any speed. So when it was moving at a snail's pace, Sam was able to throw a couple of pigs over the side and let them roll down the bank and then he would throw himself out onto the bank, where he probably had a cart waiting so he could make off with his ill-gotten gains.

But this was all to come to an end for Sam, for on his last and final excursion, there was a thick fog about the place and it was very hard to see. However, this did not deter Sam, who was obviously making a tidy profit from these excursions.

He went through the usual routine of hiding inside the freight wagon and waiting for it to be loaded up and for the side to be put up and locked.

The train pulled away as usual and started to make its slow ascent up the hill. As it did, Sam lifted and threw the pigs over the side.

Then it was his turn to jump, but as it was so foggy that he could not see that he was crossing the bridge over a main road. When he jumped, he fell to his death on the road below and was found by some passers-by who informed the RIC ('The Royal Irish Constabulary'). They came and also found the pig carcasses along the bank a bit further back down the line. They had been investigating the stolen pigs and quickly realized that this was their man.

When the culprit was identified as Sam Bán, the bridge from which he had fallen and met his demise became known as Sam's Bridge.

9

THE BRAGAN GHOST

Monaghan man Danny Aughey told me this story of a spectral encounter that took place in Co. Monaghan over sixty years ago. It is a chilling wee tale but it has a warmth to it too. Even ghosts can get lonely …

There was once a railway station in Glaslough, Co. Monaghan, which was part of the Ulster Railway in the Republic of Ireland. Glaslough Station was opened on 25 May 1858 and closed on 14 October 1957.

Now, during the late 1940s and early '50s, there were two taxis based at Glaslough Station. The fellas who drove these taxis never went too far: usually a radius of about five miles was as far as they would go. One of these taxi men was known as Ned McGovern and he was a great man to get you where you needed to be after you got off the train.

One day, in the early fifties, a man called Peter McKenna got off the train at Glaslough Station. He was what was more commonly known at the time as a 'returned Yank', which is just another way of saying someone who has returned from America. He came out of the station and, lo and behold, who was there. Only Ned McGovern, sitting in his taxi waiting to take weary travellers on the final part of their journeys.

So Peter went over to Ned's car and he tapped on the window. Ned rolled down the window and asked him where was he for. Peter told him he was for Bragan. Now, Bragan is a Monaghan townland within the Bragan mountain range (also known as the Slieve Beagh mountain range). It touches the borders of

Monaghan, Fermanagh and Tyrone and you can see views of most of Ulster and Co. Louth from it. It would be a very remote sort of a place, without much there other than gorse and grouse and very few people living there (although, funny enough, you will find a few McKennas in the area) and back then it was even more remote, but Ned agreed to take the young man to Bragan.

Well, Ned got chatting to Peter, who explained that he had been living in America for over twenty years, but he reckoned that his folks did not have long left in them so he had decided to come back and visit them. He could not believe that in all that time the place had not changed at all. Now, it was late and it was getting dark and Peter was trying to remember which lane was his. He asked Ned to stop at a lane that he thought was his.

When he went to pay, Ned said that he would wait for him to make sure that he was at the right lane, but Peter was pretty sure that it was the right one and thanked Ned for his offer, so he paid him and got out. He made his way up the little lane, which was covered in grass and could be a bit treacherous, so he had to mind his step.

Now, it was quite a walk and after a while it started to rain. Poor Peter was getting worried as the walk seemed to be longer than he had remembered it being, well over twenty years before, and he started to wish that he hadn't refused Ned's offer to wait for him.

In the distance, he saw a big holly tree, so he ran in under it for a bit of cover from the blasted rain. As he stood there, he heard footsteps coming down the lane from the other direction. He wondered who would be walking the wee lanes at this hour. Then the footsteps got closer and an old man came into his vision.

'You're home Peter,' says the auld fella.

Peter was a bit taken aback by this as he did not know who the old man was at all.

The old man continued, 'We haven't seen you in these parts for a while now. Were you away?'

Peter replied by telling him he had been away in America and that he was back to see his parents.

'How do you know me?' asked Peter.

The old man explained who he was and said that he lived near Peter and his folks. Peter remembered who the old man was then. He had heard his father speak of him and his family, but he found it strange as he thought that the old man and his people were long since gone. Peter asked him what he was doing out at this hour and who he was living with now.

'Ah, it's just meself now and I wander about the auld lanes of a night, sure 'tis better than sitting up in the house on me own,' says the old man. 'I live up there yonder, a stone's throw from here. Why don't ya come up to the house and get out of the rain for a bit and sure, I'd be grateful of the bit o' company.'

The old man pointed up the lane. Peter thought it was not a bad idea and he figured his folks had waited over twenty years, so they could wait a bit longer.

Well, they went up to the house, which was a nice wee cottage with whitewashed walls, a thatched roof and a half-door. Inside there was a lovely big turf fire with a pot hanging from a crook above it. There was a mud floor and an old rug upon it and upon that again were a couple of armchairs with cushions on them. At the side wall stood an auld settle bed, the likes of which Peter had not seen since he was a child.

There was a lovely smell of burning turf and freshly baked bread. On a table in the room, Peter could see a loaf of homemade wheaten bread and a lump of butter on a dish beside it. On the wall, he could see a picture of the Sacred Heart and an auld clock that looked like it had been telling the time since time began hung above the chimney brace.

Above the fireplace on the mantelpiece, there was an ancient-looking photograph of a young couple on their wedding day. It looked like it was taken a hundred years ago. Beside it sat an auld fiddle, a fine-looking instrument with the reflections of the flames dancing on its shiny surface.

Peter looked up at the fiddle and asked the old man if he could play.

'I can o' course,' replied the auld fella.

'Will ya play an auld tune?' asks Peter, as he had not heard the authentic old music in such a long time and, to be honest, it was one of the few things that he really missed about home.

Well, the old man told Peter to sit down by the fire and asked him if would take a wee drop of the 'holy water' or the 'Rare Old Mountain Dew', as it's better known. Well now, Peter was delighted to be in a warm dry house by the fire and, better yet, enjoying a nice glass of whiskey.

So the auld fella poured two glasses of whiskey from a very old-looking bottle and handed Peter one. Oh! It was mighty stuff. The old man put down his glass after taking a drink from it and proceeded to take down the fiddle from above the fireplace.

He played the most beautiful tunes that Peter had ever heard. It was just lovely, sitting there by the fire, enjoying a nice dram of the 'holy water' and listening to that beautiful music.

Now, it was not long before Peter fell fast asleep with the heat of the fire and the effects of the whiskey, not to mention the soothing music.

Well, Peter woke up the following morning lying on the ground, wringing wet and shivering with the cold. There was no fire and there was not even a fireplace. All he saw were the ruined remains of what had once been a fireplace. When he looked up, he saw the sky, for there was not even a roof on the house.

Peter was in an awful state of confusion, for he had vivid and clear memories of falling asleep next to an open fire and listening to music played by his host the night before.

So he picked himself and his case up off the ground and he headed on up to his father and mother's house, where he found them waiting for him. They asked where he had been as they had been expecting him the night before. He told them that he had been in the house of an old man who lived a bit further down the path, and he told them about the warm fire and the music and all the rest of it. Peter's father said that this could not have happened at all for the old man that he talked about had died almost thirty years ago.

Poor auld Peter felt a shiver go down his spine when he realised that he had spent his first night back home in the company of a ghost.

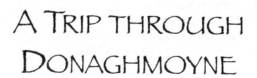

10

A Trip through
Donaghmoyne

This funny verse was written by a Dubliner called Kevin Motherway, who was a patron of the Bohemian Bar in Dublin and a council foreman.

Motherway was an avid reader and set up a book club with Ted McGeough's son Gerard.

He had never been further north of Dublin than Finglas.

The verse was intended as a comical skit on Ted and his Donaghmoyne/Co. Monaghan associates, many of whom also patronised the bar.

So get comfortable and sit back and enjoy … A trip through Donaghmoyne …

A Trip through Donaghmoyne

'From Donaghmoyne to Crossmaglen
There are no rogues but honest men.'
So goes an ancient Irish song
But I can prove those words are wrong.
Last year I passed through Donaghmoyne;
'Twas there I lost a penny coin.
Now I'm not sure, but I'll surely bet
The sods up there are searching yet;
From day to day, for hours and hours,
They seek among the weeds and flowers
That tiny little 1p coin, the miserable gets of Donaghmoyne.

And so it shows, I swear to heaven
All hungry hooers don't come from Cavan.
From North to South one emigrated,
Viewed the scene and contemplated
How to make a bob or two.
'I'll sell them drink, that's what I'll do.'
So he bought a couple of pubs
To squeeze the gold from hard-pressed Dubs.

Daily he pursues his quest
In Bohemian House and Travellers Rest
Selling Brandy, Whiskey, Stout,
The cash rolls in, the lads roll out
And he, who should the good Lord thank,
Laughs loudly going to the Bank
While I must watch my penny grow
For that Donaghmoyne man Ted McGeough.

Kevin Motherway

11

THE DEVIL AND DAVY HUTCHINSON

No collection of Irish folk stories would be complete without a tale involving 'auld Nick', better known as 'The Devil'. I came across this lovely little story in the 1997 Tydavnet Annual. It did not state who had collected it and it was very short, but it had great potential as a yarn so I took it upon myself to give it a lift and deliver to you now, with great excitement, the story of the poitín-maker Davy Hutchinson and his dealings with the Devil.

Davy Hutchinson was born in Mullindava, in the parish of Clones, Co. Monaghan, in 1848. By trade, he was a lime burner, making quicklime, but his real profession was not of a particularly noble nature, for he was a poitín-maker. That's right: he brewed the rare auld mountain dew and he was very well known for his expertise and the high quality of his produce.

He spent much of his time making the poitín and would spend around seven weeks working solidly and producing around a hundred gallons of the stuff. He called each of these marathon brewing sessions a 'go'.

Now, Davy told the people around him that he had a great friend in the Devil himself. He described him as being a little old man with a wizened face, wee eyes, with a pointy nose and ears to boot, but he was always very well dressed.

He said that he was very helpful and whenever Drumloo Lough was frozen over, the Devil would go into it and bring back 'the worm', which Davy had hidden there.

Now, for anyone who does not know what 'the worm' is, it's a long piece of copper pipe that has been formed into the shape of a coil. It is a very important part of the poitín still and is known as a 'worm' because it looks a bit like a coiled worm. Davy would dismantle his still, when he was not brewing the mountain dew, and hide its various components about the place, for the authorities were always keeping a close eye on him.

In return for such kind gestures, all the Devil would ever ask of Davy was a '*cupán*', or simply a cup of the first run of 'holy water', another fond name for poitín, which the Devil got great satisfaction from using.

There was one particular story that Davy used to tell about his old friend the Devil that always made him smile.

It all began when Davy was asked to make a 'go' by one of his neighbours. He was happy enough to do it, but there was a bit of a problem, for poor Davy was being constantly watched by the police and it was getting harder to evade them all the time.

So one particular night, he set off to find a good concealed place where he would not be found or disturbed whilst carrying out his work. Well, he searched about the place, looking for somewhere well hidden, with enough room to set up his still, when who comes out of the shadows but his old friend – yes, that's right, 'auld Nick', the Devil.

'Well, Davy, what are your troubles tonight?' says the Devil.

'Oh! There isn't much use in me telling you me troubles, Nick.'

'Why not?' asked the Devil.

Davy looked at the little old man with the sharp, wizened features and said with a great sigh, 'I fear that not even you can be of any help to me this night.'

'Ah now, Davy, let me hear them,' says the Devil.

So Davy explained to Auld Nick that he could not find a decent hiding place to make his poitín and that the police were onto him constantly and he feared that he would never be able to make his mountain dew again.

'Oh! That would be a terrible shame indeed. Imagine the world without the holy water!' said the Devil, with an evil smile on his face. 'Don't you worry now. I will sort this out for ya – that I will do surely!'

So the Devil wasted no time at all and went about making what looked like a small boat from hazel rods.

Now, when the boat was ready, the Devil told Davy to gather up all his utensils and get inside, which he did, and then Auld Nick hopped in beside him. As soon as they were aboard, Nick lifted a magic rod, tapped the prow of the boat three times with the rod and all of a sudden the vessel started to rise up into the air, right up into the clouds, where it sailed with the wind through the night sky.

As they sailed along, Davy could see the land below them and he saw Drumloo Lough and all that surrounded it. It was magnificent indeed. The boat rose higher and higher into the clouds so that Davy could no longer see anything below him but the clouds.

Well, after a while, the vessel started gradually to descend from the sky. When they landed, Davy found himself outside a magnificent castle with strange and wonderful plants growing all around it. Among these plants, there was a clearing and the Devil told Davy to carry out his work there, in peace, and that he would return for him in three days. Before he went, he left a hundred gallon bottles for Davy to fill with the precious liquid.

With that, the Devil disappeared and Davy set about his work, relaxed and free of the worry that the authorities would catch him. Now, as Davy worked away on the 'go', he was very curious to know who or what lived in the big castle above him. He figured that he had his poitín still in order and that he could leave it for a while and go see what was above in the palace. So off he went and when he got to the doors of the big castle, he gave them a good bang and there was no answer. He called out but there was still no answer. He gave the door a push and, lo and behold, didn't it swing open for him.

He went inside and he could see that the castle was fabulous, and in the centre of it he found a grand table full of every type of food and drink that you could think of and as he was very hungry he helped himself.

After he was finished, he walked through the building, taking it all in. He had never seen anything like it. In one of the rooms, he found piles of gold, silver and jewels of all descriptions. He helped himself to a few of the gold coins and a couple of large diamonds and then he thought it would be best that he get back to his still before some other type of authority was onto him.

So he went back to his still and found it all in working order. After the three days, he produced one hundred gallons of the stuff and bottled them all up, ready for the journey back.

Sure enough, after the three days, Auld Nick returned in a giant boat of hazel rods and helped Davy to load the poitín. When they were done, Davy told him that he had been to the castle and had a bite to eat and that he had found a room of magnificent treasure. He put his hand in his pocket and took out what he thought was the treasure he had taken, but when he held out his hand there was nothing but '*múnlach*' or horse manure.

'Well, that will teach you to steal fairy gold,' said the Devil, laughing. Then he looked at Davy and said, 'I think we should get out of here now, for they are all away at the moment, but they are due back very soon and they would not appreciate the likes of us about the place.'

So, with that, Davy and the Devil headed back to Davy's house and, as always, in return all the Devil requested for his help was the first cup of poitín from the 'go' – until the next time and for all eternity ...

12

CHILD OF THE FAIRY MOUNDS

Whilst collecting folklore and fairy stories in Co. Monaghan I ventured up Slieve Beagh, a mountainous area bordering Co. Monaghan, Tyrone and Fermanagh. Moved by the stories I had been already told and the mysterious yet melancholic beauty of the landscape I was inspired to write this story.

A while ago, but not too long ago, there lived a man from Slieve Beagh, Co. Monaghan, who had a great sadness in his heart, the sort of sadness that comes only from broken dreams.

Every day he would go for long walks in the surrounding hills and woods. He walked for hours as if hoping someday he would outrun his loneliness and fine peace in a place that he knew in his heart he would never find.

But then one day, as he marched through the high and wide majestic hills, a mist came down around him and he heard a sound, a sound that was like no other he had ever heard. It was beautiful, mournful and seductive. He found himself following it and it was not long before he found its source.

Sitting huddled in the undergrowth was a beautiful young woman. She looked up at him with big doe eyes that made his heart melt and all of a sudden he forgot his own sadness and was transfixed by the spell that this creature had bestowed upon him.

He fell to his knees and found himself weeping uncontrollably. The woman reached out and touched his shoulder.

'Please don't cry,' she whispered ever so gently. 'I have not much time left and you are my only salvation.' The man did not under-stand at all, but the woman explained that she had come from the fairy mounds. She had seen the man on his many walks around the hills and she had fallen in love with him and wanted to be with him.

So the Fairy King granted her this wish, but the price was losing her immortality to go and live in the world of men.

So she did this and went to find him, but her fairy form was to weak and fragile to stand up against the cold and harsh weather conditions and it was not long before she had caught a fatal fever and she was surely going to die. The man wrapped her in his coat and took her back to his house where he did his best to nurse her back to health again, but his efforts were in vain.

He realised that this creature was what he had been searching for all his life and now she was to go and be gone from him forever.

She told him that to keep the soul of a 'Siog' or Fairy alive was to share their story with as many people as possible.

So she told him her story and it was as beautiful and sorrowful as her gentle face. When she finished her eyes closed and she laid still and cold in his arms.

He took her body to the wild and mighty hills where he laid her to rest and from that day forth he went from house to house and land to land telling her story.

The people were so enchanted and transfixed by it, they would spread the word and the man was welcomed into every home to sit by the fire and tell his story in return for food and shelter.

And as he walked through those wild majestic hills he could hear his true love's voice singing ever so sweetly carried upon the wind.

He felt her warmth against his skin and her lips upon his. He was never lonely again and told her story till his own death where he would at last be united with his true love for all eternity.

And if you listen carefully to the whistling winds around Slieve Beagh, you just might hear the story of the fairy maiden whispered gently over the gorse and wild heather.

13

JOHN MARTHA AND THE LANDLORD'S GOLD

This great story was presented to me by my friend and fellow storyteller, Monaghan man Francis McCarron.

A while back in Ireland, there was a man called John Martha. John was a bit simple. As his neighbours would say, 'There was a wee want in him.' But simpleness wasn't in the breed of his people. He had a sister Kate and if you burned her for a fool, you'd have wise ashes. So where John lacked brains, Kate more than made up for him.

John and Kate were poor. They had no land, but they had a cow. Each day John would herd the cow along the long acre. For anyone who doesn't know where the long acre is, it is the free grass along the side of the road.

One day, when John was by the roadside with his cow, a pony and trap passed. Sitting on top was the landlord's agent, who had been collecting rent from the peasants of the locality. Now, it happened that when the trap had passed up the road a bit, it hit a rut in the road and bounced in the air and everything on it bounced as well. When it hit the ground again, a bag fell off the back and the driver didn't notice. He carried on his way.

But John noticed. The hungry eye sees far. He went to the spot and picked up the bag. What he found inside caused him to race home straight away. He burst through the door of the house, yelling, 'Kate, Kate, look what I found!'

'Good Lord, John, do you want to put the heart crossways in me. What has you in such a fluster?'

'The landlord's agent passed me on his cart and this bag fell off the back and it's filled with gold coins. Can we keep them, Kate? We'll be rich!'

Kate knew that what was lost would soon be looked for so her sharp mind went to work at once to see how they might keep the money. She knew John could never tell a lie, nor would he be able to keep the story to himself, so she set John a task straight away.

'We'll keep the money, for sure,' she said, 'and we'll divide it between us. You count it out and see how much there is.'

John began to count the coins.

'One … Oonnee … What comes after one, Kate?'

'Two, John, two. Everyone knows that two comes after one.'

'Oh, right so. One, two, seven, nine.'

'Och, John, John, sure, seven doesn't come after two. Three comes after two. Start again.'

'Oh? One, two, three, seven.'

'Oh, for pity's sake, John! Do you not know that four comes after three? And then five and six? Can you not count?'

'Sure, you know well I can't count, Kate. Sure, I never went to school.'

'Well,' replied Kate, 'that will have to change. You'll have to go to school tomorrow and learn your sums.'

The next day John set off to Knocknagrave school. All the scholars were in the same room and John sat with the infants. He certainly stood out amongst his classmates, which was unsurprising as he was 32 years old. The younger children teased him and made fun of him. The older ones stuck their compass points in his bum and caused him to roar out. The master slapped him for being noisy. At lunchtime, he went home to Kate.

'Kate, I don't care if I never learn to count – I'm not going back to school again.'

'Don't you worry, John, you just go back to herding your cow.'

So that's what he did. And not many days passed before he noticed a cart travelling slowly along the road and a number of men walking alongside it. They seemed to be searching the hedges and the roadway as they came along.

When they drew up to John, he recognised the landlord's agent.

'Did you lose something?' he asked politely.

'Yes, my good man,' the agent replied. 'I recently lost a bag of gold coins along the road.'

'Oh, I found them,' said John proudly.

The agent's eyes lit up with delight. 'Did you, indeed, my good man? And what did you do with them?'

'I took them home to my sister Kate.'

'Well, jump up on the cart and you and I and the members of the constabulary here shall pay her a visit.'

'Good day to you, ma'am,' said the agent, stepping into the kitchen with John and the policemen in tow. 'This young gentleman found a bag of gold coins and I am here to collect them.'

'Oh, goodness me, your honour, would you look at the state of the kitchen? Sure, if I had known you were coming … Will you have a drop of tae?'

'Not at all, ma'am, just the money and we'll be on our way.'

'What money?' asked Kate.

'The money the gentleman here found on the roadside. It's mine.'

'Och, sure, don't mind him,' said Kate. 'He's a bit simple. Sure, he comes out with all sorts of rubbish.'

The agent was taken aback and, turning to John, said, 'Well, my good man, did you or did you not find a bag of money?'

'Of course, I did,' said John. 'Kate, do you not remember?

'Remember what, John? You brought no bag of money home here.'

'I did,' protested John loudly. 'I did, I did, I did.'

'When did you bring them home?' asked Kate.

'You're bound to remember, Kate. It was the day before I went to school!'

The agent looked at John, then at the policemen and finally turned to Kate and said, 'Apologies for troubling you, ma'am. We'll be on our way.' And they left.

As for John and Kate, they lived as good a life as ever you'll live if you're smart and shrewd and honest – well, almost!

14

JOHN O'NEILL AND THE THREE DOGS

This is a fantastic tale from Monaghan collected from the 2005 Tydavnet Journal. *It is truly a spellbinding tale.*

A long time ago, near the mountains of Slieve Beagh (*Sliabh Beagh*) that straddle the border between Co. Monaghan and the counties of Fermanagh and Tyrone, there once lived a widow and her only son John. They lived on the Monaghan side of the mountain and were very poor and knew not what to do to keep themselves from starving.

They really didn't want to sell their only faithful cow, but they knew that if they were to stay alive, they would have to.

On the fair day, John set out with his cow before him.

When he reached the town, he met a man with three dogs.

'How much do you want for the cow?' John was asked.

'Twenty pounds,' said John.

'I can give you something worth much more than that,' was the reply.

'What is it?' asked John.

'My three dogs,' replied the man.

'And what use would your dogs be to me?' said John.

'Well,' was the reply, 'here is Speed. He can run so fast that nothing can catch him. Not even the wind can move so fast. Then there is Guess. He can tell you what you are thinking and inform you of future events. And this here dog is Strength. He is so strong that nothing can resist him. He is so strong that he can snap iron bars with a stroke of his paw.'

John stood in amazement.

'And now,' said the man, 'isn't that a fair exchange for your cow?'

John agreed without hesitation and they separated, one with the cow and the other with the three beautiful dogs. John now felt that he could not, without the cow or the money, return home to his mother, so he was determined to set out and seek his fortune.

With his three beautiful dogs in tow, he headed towards a forest. It was a cold winter's evening and darkness was about to fall like a black sheet over him and his dogs. John reached the forest and found shelter under some tall trees. He thought about having a wee sit-down, but in the distance he saw a light flicker in a castle, so he followed the light.

He made his way to the door of the castle and knocked. He could hear heavy footsteps approaching. The door swung open and all he could hear in a huge bellowing voice was, 'Who is there?' He was terrified because what he saw was the stuff of nightmares. Before him was a giant, a huge figure that made poor John freeze on the spot. He could feel the dogs pulling on the leads, trying to make their escape. He explained to the giant that he was tired and needed a room for the night.

The giant said, 'Yes, you can come in because you will taste delicious as breakfast in the morning.'

John continued to walk in, followed by his dogs. The dogs somehow made him feel protected.

The giant said, 'Where do you think you are going with those?'

He demanded that John leave them outside, but John said he would not enter without them.

The giant was angry, but when he heard a snarl from Strength, he soon changed his tune and said he could bring them in.

The giant, John and the dogs entered the dining room and began to eat the feast before them. John was delighted and, being a poor boy, he would never have seen such beautiful food and treats. John demanded that the dogs be fed at the table. The giant said they could be fed outdoors, but again he changed his mind after John persisted.

After they had eaten, John said he needed to rest and asked the giant if he could be brought to his room. The giant said yes, but he said he would need to put the dogs outside first. John again demanded that the dogs be treated exactly as he was.

The giant gave in to his wish once again. They entered the most luxurious room John had ever seen. He climbed up on the big bed and up jumped the dogs behind him. One at his head, one at his side and one at his feet.

John and the dogs had a peaceful night's sleep and awoke refreshed and ready for the off. The giant asked John if he would like a tour of the castle before he went. The giant said that if he agreed, he would need to tie his dogs up first. John agreed this time

and he left the dogs behind to go and look around the castle. The castle was magnificent and John was so impressed.

When they had almost finished the tour, the giant turned to John and said, 'You have seen all of my rooms but two. One is private and you cannot enter, and the other you can. Come and you can have a look.'

The giant opened the door and what John saw filled him with deep terror. Right in the middle of the floor was a huge block covered with blood and an axe beside it on the floor. On the walls hung the bodies of dead men.

'What do you think of this?' asked the giant. 'I am sick of your cheek and demands. This is where it ends. You will join these men very soon.'

He smiled at John and said, 'Kneel down, sir, and I will cut your head off. I don't think you will miss it as it's nearly useless.'

John asked to be left alone for a few minutes so he could come to terms with what was about to happen and the giant agreed. When the giant returned, John lay down and the giant cut his head off.

John was buried the next day. Guess, the dog, caught wind what was going on and said to the other two dogs, 'Do you know what happened to our master?'

'No,' they said.

'Well, the giant cut his head off and now they are on their way to bury him.'

Guess told the other two dogs that there was an enchanted well in the forest that had healing powers and if they got to it, the healing water would be able to restore their master to life.

Strength hurled himself against the cage that the three dogs were locked inside and, without exerting much effort, the three dogs were set free. Off to the forest they went in search of the healing well. They found the well and Speed immersed himself in the water and ran back to the castle as fast as he could.

By this stage, the procession had reached the graveyard. Just as they were about to lower John into the ground, Speed came out of the forest as quick as a flash.

The dog said, 'Open the coffin so I can see my master one last time.'

The giant said it was too late to do that. The gravediggers lowered him into the ground and began to cover the coffin in clay. Just then, out from the forest came Strength. He seized the giant by the neck and demanded that they open the coffin. The men did what the dog said and opened the coffin. Speed jumped in and rubbed himself all over the wound on John's neck. Guess entered the coffin and did likewise. Lastly, Strength jumped in and because his coat was shaggy and held more water, he rubbed his master's neck as best he could and to everyone's amazement John woke up and got out of the coffin.

John demanded that the giant walk back to the castle and take him to that horrible room with the dead bodies hanging on the wall. He told him to kneel down so he could cut his head off. The giant agreed, but said that he hoped he would allow him to have one last request. He asked if he could enter the private room and John agreed.

After a short time, the giant returned and kneeled down and allowed John to cut his head off. The giant was buried the next day in the grave that had been meant for John.

John was anxious to know what was in the private room. When he entered, he was surprised to see a beautiful girl sitting in an armchair. He looked at her and asked her why she was there. She told John that she was a princess and that one day while she was out in the forest a thick black fog had descended. She said that when the fog had lifted, she had no idea where she was. She was lost and on her own and frightened. The giant captured her and brought her back to the castle. He kept asking her to marry him, but she wouldn't and kept telling the giant to let her go home.

John asked her what the giant had asked her when he entered the room. The girl said that the giant told her about the enchanted well that could bring people back to life. She also told him that the giant said he was going to be beheaded and that she was to go to the healing well, fetch some water and bring him back to life. She reassured John that she was not going to do such a thing and that she couldn't care less about what came of him as long as she was free.

John asked the princess what she wished to do now.

She replied, 'I would like to go back to my people.'

So the next morning, John instructed Guess to help guide them back to where the princess belonged. Together with the other two dogs, Strength and Speed, they made their way to where the princess had once dwelled. The journey was long.

When they reached their destination and said their good-byes, John took one last look at the beautiful princess and then embarked upon the long journey back to the giant's castle, which he now took for his own.

Some time passed, until one morning Guess spoke to John and said, 'Do you remember the princess?'

John replied, 'Yes, how could I forget her?'

Guess told him that she was in terrible danger, that a ferocious lion was going to come down from the mountain and devour her unless they saved her. Guess went on to tell him that the butler from her castle promised that he would save her (because she had promised to marry her rescuer), but he would not because when the day came he would be too cowardly and he would let her be killed.

On the day the lion was to appear, John and the three dogs made their way to where the princess dwelled. When they eventually arrived, there were droves of people gathered outside to witness the happenings.

The princess was sitting next to the butler, waiting on the lion, and John and the dogs could tell from her face that she was terribly shaken and frightened.

The butler did not have an air of confidence, as expected. He looked far more afraid than the princess herself.

Just then the lion came from the mountain. He meant business. His jaws were wide open, ready to attack, and his eyes were firmly set on his prize. The crowds gasped in sheer fright and terror at what was about to happen.

When the lion pounced on his prey, the butler ran away and hid. Strength leapt up onto the lion and caught him by the throat. With one bite, he killed the lion and the creature fell dead on the ground. The crowd gasped once again, this time with utter relief for finally the princess was free. Just as the lion fell to the ground, the butler appeared again and stuck his sword into the lion, claiming that he was the one who had killed him. His intention was to make it look like he was the hero, so he would be the lucky man to marry the princess. As the princess had fainted with fright when the lion had pounced, she could not tell who had saved her and so the date for the marriage was set.

She did not love the butler, but accepted that it had been him who had rescued her and so she felt that she had no choice but to take his hand in marriage.

The wedding day arrived and this time the crowd was full of laughter and joy. Even John and the three dogs were present, but John stayed at a distance, for his heart was sad and low. He was about to witness the woman he was falling in love with marrying another man, knowing he was not the right person for her.

Just before the marriage, the princess was thinking and happened to look out of her window. Strength was sitting outside. His presence brought everything back to her and she was able to fill in the gaps and remember exactly what had happened on the day she had been rescued. She remembered the lion, the butler running away and the dog stepping in. So the princess demanded that she marry the owner of the dog and not the butler, who had pretended to be brave. What use was a man who pretended to be a hero? Anyway, she did not love him, so her heart was not true.

The butler, still lying, protested that he *was* the man who had rescued the princess, but Strength held him tight until he finally told the truth.

John and the princess married that very day and they lived happily ever after in the castle.

One day, while John and the three dogs were walking through the forest, they came by a block with an axe.

Strength said to John, 'Cut my head off.'

John was shocked and refused.

The dog said, 'If you don't, I will cut yours off.'

John said, 'I would rather that than have to kill you.'

Just as Strength was about to kill John, Guess stepped in and put his paw on John's neck. Guess told John to arise and do as Strength commanded. He told him not to be afraid and said that he would be surprised by what would happen. Strength knelt down and put his head on the block and, with closed eyes and a heavy heart, John cut the head off one of his most faithful friends.

When John opened his eyes, he saw that Strength had turned into a beautiful prince. He commanded John to cut the heads off the other two dogs, Guess and Speed. John did what he was told and they, too, turned into beautiful princes.

John gasped in astonishment.

They then told John the full story. They had been subjected to magic by the ghastly giant and taken away from their father, who was the king of Oriel. They told him how they wished to return to their father. They thanked John for his friendship and loyalty and for never giving up on them. They waved him and his new wife a sorrowful goodbye and off they set in the direction of Slieve Beagh. They were never seen again. But they say that on moonlit nights you can hear the sound of howling from the three dogs carried on the night wind.

15

HEY JOE!

This is a classic murder story which took place at the turn of the century. This story has become part of the fabric of Monaghan folklore. There was also a murder ballad written about it which is included in this volume.

If you were to look back at the brutal murders that took place on Irish soil, this one may be up there amongst the most gruesome. It took place in 1903 in Clones town, Co. Monaghan. There are some similarities between the crime and *The Butcher Boy* by Patrick McCabe, which is set in Clones town.

The man who was murdered was an egg-dealer called John Flanagan and he was visiting Clones on market day to buy lots of eggs to sell on in Belfast. The man who would eventually be con-victed of killing him was a butcher based in Clones and his name was Joe Fee. It is said that Flanagan had £80 in cash, and that he somehow came into contact with Fee and was lured to the slaugh-terhouse on Jubilee Road owned by him and his brother George.

Flanaghan took two helpers to the market with him, Patrick Moan and Joseph Connolly, and when he did not return, they searched the place. It is said that there were queues of farmers waiting to be paid by Flanaghan for their eggs and his family had to be called so they could settle the debts. While they were there, they searched every public house in Clones, thinking that as he liked a little drink, maybe he had got side-tracked and found a drinking partner and forgotten about the eggs altogether. Little did they know that the poor man was no longer on this earth.

In an article entitled 'A murder cover-up most foul' in the *Irish Times* (2014), Frank McNally states that at the trial it came out that Fee struck his victim with a 'pole-axe' and then cut his throat, like 'a pig's', before burying him in a shallow grave under quick-lime. But the peaty soil at the slaughterhouse had counteracted the lime so the body was remarkably well preserved.

It took eight months for his body to be discovered.

On the day that Flanaghan went missing, Joe Fee bought a spade from a local shop. It was said that he paid off debts and was buying better-quality livestock. I suppose it would have been said that he had come into money and this was suspicious, to say the least!

It was April when Flanaghan went missing and it wasn't until December that his body was discovered. There was a huge dung pile up outside the slaughterhouse and neighbours started to complain about its sight and smell, so Joe Fee got two local men, Albert McCoy and John Farmer, to clear it away and, lo and behold, they found a boot sticking out of the pile. They ran for the police. Head Constable McKeown came to the scene and when he tried to catch up with Joe Fee, he found him busy trying to make his escape.

Despite his escape attempt, Fee said that he was innocent and he must have been convincing because there were three murder trials before he was sentenced to death. Monaghan jurors had failed to see that he was the murderer and so the case went to Belfast, and within an hour the majority found him guilty of the murder of John Flanagan: he was sentenced to death.

During the trial, it was explained how the victim came to such a tragic end. The gruesome details were shocking and animalistic. Flanagan was treated no better than a pig.

In an online collection of 'Brutal Irish Murders' (John Baker, 2011), it states that Flanagan was stabbed with a wicked-looking pig-sticker's knife which had fallen from the corpse as it was being exhumed from its makeshift grave.

Even in the hours before his death, Fee pleaded his innocence. Just a second before he was about to be executed, he shouted 'Guilty!'

He was hung two days before Christmas in 1904 and it is believed that he had a slow, painful death because the coroner's report stated that he may have been hanging for twenty minutes, slowly choking to death.

16

THE BALLAD OF JOE FEE

This is 'The Ballad of Joe Fee'. The author is unknown.

You feeling hearted Christians, come listen unto me
While I relate the awful fate that did befall Joe Fee.
He paid his last dread penalty; words were of no avail.
He was hanged upon the scaffold high that day in Armagh Gaol.

The murder was a cruel one, no worse since time began;
The victim was an honest man, his name John Flanagan.
He came to Clones market with goods to buy and sell,
Upon a Thursday morning; the truth to you I'll tell.

He changed a cheque that morning of eighty pounds or more;
'Twas known that he had money, as he often had before,
But when the market did commence, 'twas near two, I allow,
Fee walked up, saying to Flanagan, 'I have that for you.'

They both walked off together, to Fee's house they did go;
When they entered in the slaughterhouse, Fee struck a cruel blow.
With an awful cry, poor Flanagan, he reeled unto the floor
And then the murderer cut his throat and laid him in his gore.

He buried him with candle-light; he strewed his clothes with lime,
Expecting there would be no trace of the body or the crime.
He built the dung-hill on the top and felt all was secure
Until one day two lads there came to draw away manure.

And one of them did sink a fork much deeper in the ground
And to the boy's amazement, a human foot he found;
He flung his fork in horror and off he dashed in fright
And told the police who came around and arrested Fee that night.

Two Monaghan jurors disagreed, though straight and honest men,
For the murder of John Flanagan Joe Fee was tried again;
At the winter Assizes in Belfast the jury men sat down
And gave a hearing to the case presented to the Crown.

On a cold Saturday evening, the jury took a stand,
In an hour found Fee guilty of killing this young man
And everyone within the court sat mute and held their breath
As the judge, he put on his black cap and sentenced Fee to death.

And then the fatal day arrived when Fee was doomed to die
In expiation of his crime upon the gallows high;
And while God's mercy he did crave as the death-bell it did toll,
We will say, God rest John Flanagan and have mercy on his soul.

17

THE ROSSMORE
BANSHEE

The Banshee plays a significant role in Irish folklore. It was to my great delight that I found a Banshee story associated with Co. Monaghan. Whilst speaking to various Monaghan folk, I was told of 'The Rossmore Banshee'.

The magnificent Rossmore Castle was situated on the outskirts of Monaghan town, Co. Monagahan. The area is now known as Rossmore Park. Rossmore was built for Warner Westenra (1765– 1842), the 2ⁿᵈ Baron Rossmore. The Westenras, who were of Dutch descent, had inherited the title upon the death of the 1ˢᵗ Baron, Robert Cunninghame (1726–1801), whom this story is based on.

The house was the main residence of the Westenras until the 1950s, when dry rot and disrepair forced the family to move to another property on the grounds.

Eventually, the ill-fated house could no longer be maintained and it was demolished in 1974. Although the Rossmore Mausoleum still stands in Rossmore Park …

I found this story in *Personal Sketches of his Own Times* by Sir Jonah Barrington, in which there is an account of a ghostly experience Sir Jonah Barrington (1757–1834) and his wife Catherine, Lady Barrington, had when they were invited by General Robert Cunninghame (1726–1801), 1ˢᵗ Baron Rossmore of Monaghan, to his home, Mount Kennedy House in Co. Wicklow.

Barrington, who was an Anglo-Irish lawyer, judge and politician, was a good friend of Rossmore, who was commander-in-chief of His Majesty's Forces in Ireland from 1793 to 1796.

Fortune had favoured Lord Rossmore at every turn. Not only had he been eminently successful in his military vocation; he had been equally fortunate in marriage and finance. The lady with whom he had fallen in love returned his affections and, on their marriage, brought him a rich dowry.

It was partly with her money that he purchased the estate of Mount Kennedy for £19,691 0s 10d, from Elizabeth Barker, in 1769. It comprised of 10,000 Irish acres.

Not very far from Mount Kennedy, in the centre of what was called the golden belt of Ireland, stood Dunran, the residence of the Barringtons. Lord Rossmore and the Barringtons were practically neighbours.

This is what Sir Jonah had to say about Wicklow, in his own words:

> The scenery of Wicklow is doubtless on a very minor scale, quite unable to compete with the grandeur and immensity of continental landscape; even to our own Killarney it is not comparable; but it possesses a genial glowing luxury, where of more elevated scenery is often destitute. In the world its beauties seem alive. It blooms, it blossoms, the mellow climate extracts from every shrub a tribute of fragrance wherewith the atmosphere is saturated, and through such a medium does the refreshing rain descend to brighten the hues of the evergreens. The site of my sylvan residence, Dunran, was nearly in the centre of the golden belt, about fifteen miles from the capital; but owing to the varied nature of the country, it appeared far more distant. Bounded by the beautiful glen of the Downs, at the foot of the magnificent Bellevue, and the more distant Sugarloaf mountain.

Barrington loved to visit Lord Rossmore. As he put it:

> One of the greatest pleasures I enjoyed whilst resident at Dunran, was visiting the near abode of the late Lord Rossmore. He was what

may be called a remarkably fine old man, quite the gentleman, and when at Mount Kennedy quite the country gentleman.

He lived in a style few people can attain to. His table, supplied by his own farms, was fit for the Viceroy himself yet was ever spread for his neighbours.

In a word, no man ever kept a more even hand in society than Lord Rossmore, and no man was ever better repaid by universal esteem. Had his connections possessed his understanding, and practised his habits, they would probably have found more friends when they wanted them.

The story begins one afternoon in August of 1801, when Lord Rossmore was attending the vice-royalty of Earl Hardwick in the drawing room at Dublin Castle. It was then that Lord Rossmore met Lady Barrington. He had been organising one of his weekly parties, which were held at Mount Kennedy, and eagerly invited her and her husband to come to the house party at Mount Kennedy the following day.

'My little farmer,' said he, addressing her by her pet name, 'when you go home, tell Sir Jonah that no business is to prevent him from bringing you down to dine with me to-morrow. I will have no ifs in the matter—so tell him that come he must!'

Lady Barrington promised and the following day saw her and Sir Jonah at Mount Kennedy. That night, at about midnight, they retired to rest and towards two in the morning Sir Jonah was awakened by a strange sound.

It first occurred at short intervals and sounded like neither a voice nor an instrument, for it was softer than any voice and wilder than any music and seemed to float in the air, moving about from one spot to another.

To quote Sir Jonah:

We retired to our chamber about twelve; and towards two in the morning, when I was awakened by a sound of a very extraordinary nature. I don't know wherefore, but my heart beat forcibly; the sound became still more plaintive, till it almost died in the air; when a sudden change, as if excited by a pang, changed its tone; it seemed descending.

I felt every nerve tremble: it was not a natural sound, nor could I make out the point from whence it came. At length I awakened Lady Barrington, who heard it as well as myself. She suggested that it might be an Æolian harp; but to that instrument it bore no resemblance—it was altogether a different character of sound. My wife at first appeared less affected than I; but subsequently she was more so. We now went to a large window in our bedroom, which looked directly upon a small garden underneath. The sound seemed then, obviously, to ascend from a grass plot immediately below our window. It continued loudly.

Lady Barrington requested I would call up her maid, which I did, and she was evidently more affected than either of us.

The sounds lasted for more than half an hour. At last a deep, heavy, throbbing sigh seemed to come from the spot, and was shortly succeeded by a sharp, low cry, and by the distinct exclamation, thrice repeated, of 'Rossmore!—Rossmore!—Rossmore!' I will not attempt to describe my own feelings.

At this point, Sir Jonah was indeed terrified, as were Lady Barrington and her maid. The terrible wailing voice screamed out Rossmore's name. The maid ran screaming from the window and Lord Barrington urged his wife to return to bed in an attempt to establish calm.

Again, in his own words:

The maid fled in terror from the window, and it was with difficulty I prevailed on Lady Barrington to return to bed; in about a minute after the sound died gradually away until all was still.

When it had all calmed down, Lady Barrington begged her husband not to tell a soul about what they had witnessed as she feared they would be the laughing stock of the place.

Sir Jonah recounts:

Lady Barrington, who is not so superstitious as I, attributed this circumstance to a hundred different causes, and made me promise that I would not mention it next day at Mount Kennedy, since we should be thereby rendered laughing-stocks.

Sir Jonah promised his wife that he would not utter a word, but this was obviously not his intention, as I would never have come across this story otherwise.

He went on to say:

At length, wearied with speculations, we fell into a sound slumber. Then about seven the next morning a strong rap at my chamber-door awakened me. The recollection of the past night's adventure rushed instantly upon my mind, and rendered me very unfit to be taken suddenly on any subject. I went to the door, when my faithful servant, Lawler, exclaimed, on the other side, 'Lord, sir!'

'What is the matter?' said I hurriedly.

'Oh, sir!' ejaculated he, 'Lord Rossmore's footman was running past the door in great haste, and told me in passing that my Lord, after coming from the Castle, had gone to bed in perfect health (Lord Rossmore, though getting on in years, had always appeared to be very healthy, and Sir Jonah had never once heard him complain that he was unwell), but that about half after two this morning, his own man, hearing a noise in his master's bed (he slept in the same room), went to him, and found him in the agonies of death; and before he could alarm the other servants, all was over!'

Sir Jonah remarks that Lord Rossmore was actually dying at the moment when Lady Barrington and he heard the voice calling his name. He adds that he cannot account for the sounds with any reasonable explanations.

This is what Barrington wrote about the whole experience:

I conjecture nothing. I only relate the incident as un-equivocally matter of fact.

Lord Rossmore was absolutely dying at the moment I heard his name pronounced. Let sceptics draw their own conclusions; perhaps natural causes may be assigned; but I am totally unequal to the task.

Atheism may ridicule me; orthodoxy may despise me; bigotry may lecture me; fanaticism might mock me; yet in my very faith I would seek consolation. It is, in my mind, better to believe too much than too little; and that is the only theological crime of which I can be fairly accused.

Lord Rossmore, 1st Baron Rossmore of Monaghan died on the 6 August 1801 at approximately 2 a.m.

This story was covered many years later in a book called *The Banshee*, published in 1907, by Elliott O'Donnell (27 February 1872–8 May 1965), a renowned Victorian ghost hunter and authority on the supernatural, who claimed to have seen ghosts and to have been attacked by them.

O'Donnell claimed that he was unsure whether the phantom that took Rossmore was a Banshee, as Rossmore was of Scottish descent and one has to be of pure Irish descent to have a Banshee.

But maybe you should visit Rossmore Mausoleum when the evenings get a bit shorter and listen carefully to the whispering voices carried by the wind …

18

THE BANSHEE

The following poem is known as a 'keen' and is taken from Fairy
Legends and Traditions of the South of Ireland, *Volume I (1825),
by Thomas Crofton Croker (1798–1854).*

*'Keening' is the Irish term for a wild song or lamentation poured
forth over a dead body by certain mourners employed for the purpose.
The reader will find a paper on this subject with musical notation for
the Irish funeral lamentation in the fourth volume of the* Transactions
of the Royal Irish Academy. *The following verses, translated from
a popular keen, are quoted because of the presence of the Banshee in
the keen, which was composed for a young man named Ryan, whose
mother is the narrator.*

Maidens sing no more in gladness
To your merry spinning wheels;
Join the keener's voice of sadness,
Feel for what a mother feels.

See the space within my dwelling;
'Tis the cold blank space of death.
'Twas the Banshee's voice came swelling
Slowly o'er the midnight heath.

Keeners, let your song not falter;
He was as the hawthorn fair.

Lowly at the virgin's altar
Will his mother kneel in prayer.

Prayer is good to calm the spirit
When the keen is sweetly sung;
Death though mortal flesh inherit,
Why should age lament the young?

'Twas the Banshee's lonely wailing –
Well, I knew the voice of death,
On the night wind slowly sailing
O'er the bleak and gloomy heath

19

HOLY WATER

This chilling tale is based on a true story that children of Monaghan still tell to this day.

The legend of the sleepwalking nun, Sister Mary Keough, dates back to 1875. It has been passed down through the years and is still part of the oral tradition in Co. Monaghan today.

The Sisters of St Louis, based in Monaghan town, were well respected and held in high esteem in the vicinity and surrounding areas, so if the facts of the following incident had surfaced, it would have brought shame and embarrassment on the order.

The story is about a nun who takes her own life in 1875. A nun committing suicide would have been a catastrophe, so by saying that the nun came to her death by accident while sleepwalking makes the ordeal more acceptable and somehow romanticises the event.

Sister Mary Keough had been in her order for twelve years, since she was 18 years old, so she was still a young woman when she took her own life at 30. It is not known why she did so. Some speculate that she wanted to leave the convent, some say she met a man, but this is all just hearsay and these speculations may have been added to the story for effect.

It is believed that two months before her death, her behaviour changed. The women around her began to notice the changes, especially her superioress, Sister Mary Beale. It is said that Mary Keough became depressed and was eating less. It was obvious to those who knew her that she had given up; apparently Sister Mary Beale said to the reverend at the time, L.J. O'Neill, that poor Mary had been absent from her duties and that she was concerned for her well-being.

Mary told someone that she had a headache that wouldn't go away, so Mary Beale called Dr Ross and an appointment was made for early in the new year. The morning of the appointment came and Mary was nowhere to be found. The grounds were searched and a cape was found beside the water's edge of the convent lake.

Poor Mary's body was found in the water. She was dressed only in her nightdress. This may have been the inspiration for the sleep-walking story that was released afterwards by the sisters.

The official verdict was that Sister Mary Keough came to her death on 6 January 1875 from drowning while labouring under temporary insanity, but it would have been considered too contro-versial for the convent to tell the truth, so they made up their own version of events.

In *Melancholy Madness: A Coroner's Casebook*, Michelle McGoff-McCann (Mercier Press, 2003) writes about Sister Mary Keough and how her inquest told a different story to the one people would have told long ago.

Many variations of the sleepwalking-nun story exist and although the truth is easier to understand in today's society, it is amazing that an order of nuns would rather lie than say what had actually happened, although it is true that many more tragic stories about cover-ups in the Church have come to light of late.

One story holds that when Sister Mary was sleepwalking out by the lake near the convent, some of her fellow nuns followed her, but couldn't get to her in time. She walked into the water, but, lo and behold, to the shock and amazement of her fellow sisters, she proceeded to walk effortlessly upon the water, treading on it like she would on the surface of a road. When the nuns called out her name, she woke up, startled, and fell into the lake and drowned.

The incident was made to look like a miracle or supernatural event that was interrupted by human intervention.

Did the nuns all gather and decide on this story? Did they want to make her all-divine and make the story almost sacred so that no one would question it?

This would have been very easy to do almost 150 years ago because the Catholic Church had a vice-like grip on people's thinking at the time.

Why didn't they just say that she was sleepwalking and fell into the lake? That would have been tragic enough, but by putting the story beyond human comprehension, they sought to avoid any sort of controversy or questioning.

Ironically, this strategy backfired as the story became local folklore and, almost 150 years later, children still talk of the ghostly nun who wanders around Monaghan town by night.

Sadly, the truth is that Sister Mary Keough died after taking her own life in Monaghan town in 1875 because she didn't have anyone she could confide in about the phantoms that were haunting her.

20

SKELTON'S INN

This is a story about Monaghan's very own Procrustes (an ancient Greek villain who owned a murderous bed) or Sweeney Todd (from Sweeney Todd: The Demon Barber of Fleet Street*).*

He was a man called Skelton, who was an innkeeper from Tydavnet, and this is his chilling tale.

A long time ago, the village of Tydavnet was famous for its many fairs and markets and people came from all around to buy and sell their wares. It was a very exciting and popular place and it was all the more exciting if you owned a business there as you stood to benefit from all the reckless spending.

Well, there was no one like Skelton to benefit from the money pouring in and he made sure that he did. He owned an inn in Tydavnet known as Skelton's Inn, which was considered to be the best in the village. Skelton had plenty of money and was always accommodating the people who came to the fairs by serving them food and drink and putting them up in his fine establishment.

Now, during the day, when trading was at its most ferocious, Skelton would watch to see how well it was all going. He would figure out who the wealthy merchants and buyers were and he would also figure out who was from distant parts of the country and then he would determine who was wealthy and from far away – now, they were the clients that he was interested in. For when they would come to his inn in the evening, after they had made all the bargains, he would talk to the wealthiest one and offer them his best room, with the finest bed, for the night.

Well, after a long day at the fair and with their skinfull of drink, the merchants would always agree rather than having to face a long and treacherous journey home at night on unlit country roads.

So, during the night, when the unwary wayfarer was sleeping in his big comfortable bed, the bed itself would tip up, a mechanism that was, no doubt, made possible by some sinister lever operated by Skelton himself. The occupant of the bed would be tipped out and dropped into a cellar below the inn, where Skelton kept a great and ferocious hound that would attack and kill the unfortunate guest. Skelton would then relieve the dead man of his wealth and earnings from his day at the fair and this is how he came to be so very wealthy.

Now, this went on for many years until it all came to a head when a wealthy merchant from Co. Meath was persuaded to stay the night at Skelton's Inn.

Well, this merchant had a dog that he loved very much and would bring everywhere with him and he would often choose the dog's comfort and well-being over his own. It was this uncondi-tional love for his dog that was to save the man's life. For, on the fateful night that he spent in Skelton's Inn, he allowed his dog to sleep on the bed and he himself slept on the floor. So when the bed was tipped up, the dog slid down into the cellar and its owner was awoken by all the commotion and barking below him. Well, he raised the alarm and the authorities were called and Mr Skelton was hanged for his diabolical activities.

Now, one would think that this was the end of the story, but it has been said that on dark, windy nights around the old graveyard in Tydavnet, a great hound with eyes that burn like red coals can be seen galloping through the night, howling and snarling like a demon, with a great chain around its neck. It is believed that this is Skelton's hound.

S told me that he once asked his own father if he had ever seen a ghost and his father related this story to him …

His father said that he had never seen the hound, but that Francie's grandfather had. It all began when there was a wake taking place in the locality. Francie's grandfather and his friend and neighbour Patrick Falamie went to Tydavnet to get beer for the

wake. It was getting dark and so they were following the Mass path to the pub, which led them through the graveyard.

They went inside the graveyard and Francie's grandfather sat on the wall at the back of the graveyard while the neighbour, Patrick Falamie, went over to the pub to get the beer for the wake. Now, the strange thing about the old Tydavnet graveyard is the fact that on the outside there is an 8-foot drop from the wall, but inside the churchyard at the back, it is only a foot from the top of the wall to the ground. Apparently this is due to the overcrowding in the graveyard.

Now, Patrick went into the pub and while Francie's grandfather was sitting on the wall, he heard the great rattle of a chain and out of nowhere a great hound ran up through the centre of the graveyard and through the gate at the front of the cemetery.

Well, he thought nothing of it, for it was not uncommon to see large dogs about the place. But he said that Patrick Falamie came out of the pub carrying a crate of beer with both hands and came over to the gate of the graveyard and shouted, 'Mick, will ya open the gate there now!' So Mick hopped down and opened the gate for Patrick and they both walked back through the cemetery to the wake.

Well, Mick thought no more of it until the next day, when he was at the funeral in the cemetery and he looked at the gate that he had seen the dog run through. The bars of the gate were very close together so a large dog could not have gotten through them. The wall either side of the gate was 8-foot high, so the beast could not have jumped over that. And, of course, the gate was shut as Patrick had asked him to open it for him.

Well, Francie's grandfather reckoned that he had seen the ghost of Skelton's terrible hound in the old cemetery and was slow to go in there after dusk again, and certainly wouldn't venture in again during the night.

21

St Davnet

It has become a tradition of mine to write about a saint for each of my collections of folklore. When I wrote Down Folk Tales, *I had a great time writing about St Donard, who supposedly still resides on top of Slieve Donard in the Mourne Mountains, and for* Kildare Folk Tales *I had the wonderful experience of writing about St Bridgid and the fantastic tales that surround her.*

It was explained to me that Tydavnet gets its name from Saint Davnet, 'the patron saint of madness'. Well, as you can imagine, I was intrigued when I heard this and now I would like to tell you her story.

In St Joseph's Church in Carrickmacross, there is a set of magnificent original stained-glass windows by the legendary artist Harry Clarke. One of the windows depicts a terrifying yet beautiful adaption of St Davnet's story.

Davnet (Irish: *Damhnait*; also known as Damnat or Dympna) was a nun who is said to have lived and died on Slieve Beagh, Co. Monaghan, at Tydavnet (from '*Tí nDamnat*' or '*Tigh Damhnait*', meaning 'house of Damnat').

There are different stories of Saint Davnet. Some say she was a virgin nun and the founder of a church or monastery. Others say she was the daughter of a pagan chieftain who lived in Clogher, Co. Tyrone, but that she herself converted to Christianity.

She is also considered to be the same person as St Dympna, the patron saint of Geel in Flanders. This was stated by John Colgan in the mid-seventeenth century, who claimed that they were the same person. However, this was challenged by George Petrie and John

O'Donovan of the antiquities division of the Ordnance Survey (*c.* 1830/40s) who stated that they were two very different people.

A tenth-century ornamental pilgrim's staff, the *bachall Damhnait,* said to have belonged to her has been preserved. In the past, it was used to see if someone was telling the truth; it was, in other words, a lie detector. It can now be found on display in the National Museum of Ireland in Dublin.

The feast day of St Davnet is 14 June. Although the feast day of St. Dympna is 15 May.

Well, that is what I like about Irish saints: they are claimed by so many people and there are always arguments about their origins and where they found their end, if at all. There is still an ongoing debate about whether St Bridgid hails from Co. Kildare or Co. Louth.

Well, this is the story that I heard about St Davnet and I feel that it is definitely worthy of inclusion in a collection of folk tales …

Davnet was the beautiful daughter of Damon, a petty King of Oriel (*Airgíalla,* which was a medieval Irish over-kingdom: Oriel was the collective name for the confederation of tribes that formed the over-kingdom). Damon's kingdom was in Clogher in the county of Tyrone, but the burial ground for many of the royalty of the time was in Tydavnet and that is where the 'Tydavnet Discs' were found. They are two beautiful and ornate gold discs, which are now kept at the National Museum in Dublin and are considered to be amongst Ireland's greatest treasures.

Davnet's mother died when she was a young woman in the prime of her life. Davnet was heartbroken, as was her father Damon, who was an obsessive and uncompromising man. He would not accept his wife's death at all and it did not take long for his grief to turn to anger and resentment. He commanded his Druids to bring her back to life and when they could not, he had some of them executed. There was a lot of fear in the kingdom for the people knew that their king would stop at nothing to get what he wanted.

Davnet was appalled by her father's behaviour for she had recently converted to Christianity and was greatly opposed to his pagan beliefs. As a last resort, the king ordered his men to travel the length and breadth of the country and find him a woman who looked exactly like the wife he had lost, for he wished to re-marry and would only do so with a virgin who resembled his deceased wife.

Well, as you can imagine, women from all over the country jumped at the opportunity to marry a rich and powerful king. It was like an ancient Irish version of *Cinderella*, with all these maidens flocking to the king, offering themselves up for marriage.

But none of them could fit the bill and the king was furious. He was determined to marry a woman who looked like his dead wife and that was that.

Now, his Druids were starting to panic and they were looking at each other as if to say, 'Who will be the next one to lose his head over this?'

So they came up with a cunning plan to save their necks and take themselves out of the picture. They muttered and mumbled amongst themselves, as Druids always did, and then, eureka, they came up with a brilliant plan altogether. They decided that the king should marry his daughter Davnet, for she was the spitting image of her dear, departed mother.

So the head Druid, who was lucky to still have his head, went to see the king and passed on the fantastic solution that he and his fellow Druids had come up with. Well now, the king was delighted. He thought that this was a fantastic plan altogether and congratulated the Druid on his great thinking and sent him on his way to pass on the good news to his daughter.

Well, as you can imagine, Davnet was not impressed at all with this decision as she was both a Christian and a decent woman. She was annoyed, but she knew she had to tread carefully as her father was neither the most rational nor the most reasonable of men. She knew that to act hastily could be very dangerous, so she agreed to think about it for forty days, after which she would make her final decision. At least this would give her time to come up with some plan to get out of this compromising situation.

The initial plan was to get as far away from her insane father with her priest Bernard, or Gerebernus, and the pair of them would find safety far from the mad king.

She and Gerebernus went over the mountain of Slieve Beagh and stopped in the townland of Drumfurrer, in the parish of

Truagh, Co. Monaghan. When they got there, they were weak with the thirst and Davnet asked some of the local people for a drink of water, but the people of Drumfurrer knew who she was. They were terrified of her father and refused to give her a drink for fear of the repercussions they might suffer.

Well, Davnet was furious and she put a curse on the townland of Drumfurrer, that it may never have water in it, and since then there never has never been a spring well in Drumfurrer.

So the princess and her priest headed away from the townland of Drumfurrer and on across the mountain of Slieve Beagh and came to the townland of Caldavnet, where she got a drink at a spring well there, which is now known as Saint Dympna's Well.

After that, she went on to the village of Tydavnet. When herself and Gerebernus got there, she wanted to light a fire so that they could rest for the night. She approached the local blacksmith and asked him for some hot coals so that she could light a fire. The roguish blacksmith thought that this would be a great opportunity to play a trick on a woman, so he told her to hold out her apron like a wee hammock and he would put the hot coals into it, so that she could carry them away. This is what she did, but when he dropped the coals into her apron, he was surprised to see that they did not burn through.

He was very excited by what he saw and told everyone he met in the village of the miracle he had witnessed, and when he did word got around that she must have some great power or be one of the holy people that were going about the place, and of course it was well known that such people had the power to cure all sorts of illnesses.

So Davnet was called to a house where a sick woman was on her deathbed and she was asked to help her. Well, Davnet went to the house and laid her hands on the woman's head and said some words. The woman was cured and Tydavnet was named after the house where Davnet performed her miracle ('Tydavnet' meaning 'house of Davnet').

Davnet then went on to Lavey in Co. Cavan, where there is a Saint Dympna's church and at this church there is a stone, which bears the hoof prints of her horse, which were left behind when she had to jump over a river to escape her father, who was onto her by then and catching up with her.

She and Gerebernus continued on to the wes, to Achill Island
in Co. Mayo, to a place called Kildavnet (*Cill Damhnait*), which
is located on the south-eastern shore of Achill Island and overlooks
the waters of Achill Sound. The place name literally means 'the
small church of Davnet' and refers to the church that Davnet built
there. However, the place is better known as the home of its most
famous inhabitant, the legendary pirate queen Granuaille (Grace
O'Malley, 1530–1603), but that is another story.

The two were safe on Achill Island for a while until her father
found out about their whereabouts. He and his group of choice
warriors were on their scent again, so poor Davnet and Gerebernus
had to take a boat from the island in order to evade their pursuers.
From there, they went to Belgium. They went to Antwerp first and
then fled to the Flemish countryside until they reached Geel.

In Geel, they lived beside a chapel of St Martin. They stayed
until Damon discovered their whereabouts once again. Apparently,
he had been told by an innkeeper in a nearby village that they
had passed through his inn. He had recognised the coins used by
Damon from seeing Davnet use them. When Damon asked which
direction they went in, the innkeeper raised his hand and as soon
as he did this his arm froze. This must have been some divine pun-
ishment for his betrayal of Davnet. It was not long before the king
caught up with his daughter and her priest.

He claimed that he wanted to renew his offer, but seeing that all
was in vain and seeing that Davnet could not be persuaded, he told
his servants to kill the priest. When this did not convince her, he
ordered his men to behead Davnet, but they refused, so in a fit of
rage, Damon himself cut off the head of his own daughter.

The people of Geel who witnessed this atrocity decided that
the king must be insane. After they buried both Davnet and
Gerebernus, the people of Geel went to her grave to pray for the
souls of the insane and to ask for cures for mental illnesses. It was
because of this that St Davnet, or St Dympna, became the patron
saint of insanity.

Over the years, a large number of pilgrims have travelled to the
town of Geel to pay homage to St Davnet and ask for her cures.

As both Davnet and Gereburnus were canonised and declared
saints, it was decided that their corpses should be exhumed from

their graves and put in sarcophagi in a cave, where they were later found. Some say that their bodies were put in the sarcophagi by the angels themselves for they could not figure out where the stone for the tombs had come from.

Now, word had spread that the relics of the two saints were housed in Geel and there was a lot of money in holy relics, then as now, so a group of thieves and robbers from Xanten in Germany went to steal the bones of the two saints. The thieves managed to get away with the bones of Gerebernus, which are still housed in Xanten, Germany.

Luckily the bones of Saint Dympna were recovered and they are kept safely at St Dympna's church in Geel, Belgium. Every five years, they are processed through the streets of Geel in a silver shrine and pilgrims come from all over the world to take part in the procession and the nine-day pilgrimage.

When people came for the pilgrimage, there was very little in the way of accommodation, so the local people offered to take care of many of them while they were there. This was the first example of community care for the mentally ill and it was happening centuries before it started to be practised elsewhere. A hospital for the mentally ill was built in Geel and today it contains a brilliant state-run sanatorium.

Most pilgrims to Geel are still able to board with neighbourhood farmers and families, who become like 'foster families' for them. They help with the household chores or whatever work needs to be done on the farm – or, at least, they do as much as they are capable of doing. This has been happening in Geel for centuries with great success.

Now, to finish off this story, I would like to take this opportunity to tell you a wee tale about St Davnet, which was told to me by Francis McCarron.

Francis once knew a man from Tydavnet in Co. Monaghan called Leo Lord, who emigrated to America and joined the American army. He went on to fight in the Battle of the Bulge in Belgium during the Second World War.

Leo was a great believer in St Davnet and when he was in Belgium during the war, he visited St Dympna's church in Geel and paid his respects. In fact, he claimed that it was this very saint that saw him through the war.

Leo had told Francis that when he was a young boy growing up in Tydavnet, he had served as an altar boy and after one Sunday Mass, when he was changing out of his vestments, he heard something hit the ground with a thud outside the sacristy door. So he opened the door and, to his shock and bemusement, he saw the head of a beautiful young woman on the ground. As he gazed on, it melted away before his eyes. Leo believed that he had seen the head of St Davnet, or St Dympna, and since then he kept her as his spiritual companion and guide through life.

So that is the story of St Davnet. Whether it is true or not and whether Dympna and Davnet are the same person is up for speculation. But then, how else would you explain the links between Tydavnet and Geel?

Whatever the case may be, you must always remember never to let the truth get in the way of a good story …

22

THE HOLY GHOST

*This story was told to me by native Monaghan man Danny Aughey.
It is set during the Irish War of Independence or the Tan War (1919–
1921). This was a guerrilla war fought between the Irish Republican
Army (or the Old IRA) and the British security forces in Ireland,
namely the Black and Tans, hence 'The Tan War'.*

*The Black and Tans, officially known as the Royal Irish
Constabulary Special Reserve, were a ruthless force of violent men who
relied more on brutality than skill and training.*

*This story is as haunting for the brutal reality of its setting as for its
supernatural elements.*

There was a man from Glaslough (meaning 'Green Lake', this
is where Castle Leslie can be found) in Co. Monaghan who was
fighting with the Old Irish Republican Army during the Irish War
of Independence.

Now, he had managed to escape from a group of Black and Tans
that had captured his platoon. So, he was on the run and had to
travel by night and sleep by day. He slept wherever he could, in
hay sheds and wooded areas and if there were any safe houses, sure,
that was all the better. But he had to keep moving. As he had to
keep to the fields and off the roads, travel was very slow and he
could not travel too far for too long.

Well now, he was somewhere between Glaslough and Emmyvale
when he saw a priest he recognised and knew he could trust, so he
approached the priest, who was very pleased to see him and said
that he had not seen him about the place for a brave while. He

asked the young man where he had been and he told him that he was on the run and had to lay low for a while in hay sheds and safe houses and he was running out of places to hide from the Tans and informers.

Well, the priest was only too happy to help him and told him there was a place at Donagh chapel where he could stay, for they had built rooms over the chapel for the priests as they could not afford a parochial house at the time.

Now, this seemed like a great idea altogether and the young man was very grateful and relieved that he would have a safe place to stay for a while. So, the priest took him there and showed him the two rooms over the chapel. There was a wee kitchen and the priest said he would make him up a bed too. Sure, the young man was delighted. The priest gave him a key to get to the rooms and said

that he could keep it, but that he must keep the door locked at all times.

So the young fugitive came and went as he pleased and all was well. One evening when he got back from one of his late excursions, he decided that he would go into the chapel below and say a couple of prayers to give thanks for how things had improved for him.

He knelt down in one of the aisles and put his head in his hands and began to pray. But it was not long before he fell asleep in the peaceful chapel. He was woken up by a bell ringing and when he looked up he saw a priest standing on the altar, all in white. The priest turned around and asked if there was anyone in the congregation who could serve Mass and the young man, who had been an altar boy, offered to serve the Mass.

Now, at that time, the priest would have stood on the altar with his back to the congregation and said the Mass in Latin and that is exactly what happened that night in Donagh chapel.

When the Mass was over, the mysterious priest turned around and thanked the young man for serving Mass.

He told the young man that he had been coming to the chapel for over sixty years and that he could never get anybody to serve Mass, so he was very grateful.

With that, to the young man's surprise, the priest vanished right before his eyes. Quietly the man turned and went on up to his room, content in the knowledge that he had helped some old ghost find peace at last on that lonely night in Donagh chapel.

23

THE GRAVEYARD BRIDE

The chilling story of the graveyard bride has its origins in Errigal Truagh graveyard, Co. Monaghan. It is a wonderful ghost story. The writer William Carleton wrote a poem based on it. The graveyard bride conjures up both the imagery and eeriness of an Edgar Allan Poe classic.

There are few greater superstitions and fears in Ireland than those linked with death.

If a magpie comes to your door and looks at you, it is a sure sign of death and when a swarm of bees suddenly quits the hive, it is a sign that death is hovering near the house. Stop all clocks at the time of death to confuse the Devil and give the soul time to reach heaven. Cover all mirrors at the time of a death in the house, or the soul of the deceased will become trapped in the mirror. In Ireland, the dead are carried out of the house feet first in order to prevent the spirit from looking back into the house and calling upon other members of the family to follow him.

These are just a few of the superstitions that some people in Ireland still believe to this day. Most of them have been passed down from generation to generation.

The 'Demon Bride', also known as the graveyard bride or the phantom bride, is a folkloric figure that goes about stealing the life force from hapless mourners. The stories about her (there are a few male equivalents also) would put the fear of God into anyone.

Graveyards are the perfect setting for a good ghost story. Many won't walk past them or visit them after dark. Some recall seeing shadows or hearing voices late at night. Some say that these voices are the souls gathering together. Lots of stories from Irish folklore are based on the dead and their resting place. But no story I have come across is as chilling as the story of the graveyard bride that roams a medieval graveyard in Co. Monaghan.

Errigal Truagh medieval church and graveyard is one of the most ancient religious sites in Ulster. It is believed to have been a

site of worship as far back as early Christian times. The graveyard was used for burials into the present century, but the church next to it was dismantled in 1835.

The graveyard is acclaimed for its distinctively carved eighteenth-century headstones and there is a holy well that attracted generations of pilgrims until the nineteenth century. People can still visit the well to this day.

The church is dedicated to Saint Mellan, or Muadan, and the graveyard has one of the most important collections of decorated headstones in Ireland. According to the Monaghan tourism website, the headstones in the graveyard are carved in a distinctive south Ulster style. Many of the headstones feature the five mortality symbols: skulls, long bones, coffins, bells and hourglasses.

People might come to the holy well for a drop of holy water to bring to the sick or elderly, and some might come to photograph the ancient headstones, but one thing is for sure: no one comes to meet the graveyard bride. I am sure funerals in this graveyard were not well attended when word got out of the spirit's presence – it is believed that if a beautiful women (or handsome man) approaches you after a funeral and arranges a date with you, then it will not be long before you too are put into the ground.

There are many versions of the same story, but sadly they all end the same way – in death.

One version of the story holds that when a funeral takes place in the graveyard, an entity is present. It manifests itself as a woman and to the human eye appears to be a living, breathing human being. This 'woman' mingles with the congregation and so to those in attendance, she would not look out of place. She approaches the last person to leave the funeral (if the hanger-on happens to be a man) and she goes about setting a date when she and the mortal can meet before vanishing into thin air. The date they set is the date the man will die.

Another version I heard from a person in the locality held that the lady is meant to have a charmed passion and comes with a promise to meet in the churchyard on a month from that day. The promise is sealed by a kiss, which results in a deadly stain on the skin of the receiver. It might even be his last kiss. A fatal kiss.

In *Banshees, Beasts and Brides from the Sea: Irish Tales of the Supernatural* (Appletree Press, 1996), Bob Curran writes the story of the graveyard bride. In his detailed description, he states that if the person is a man, then the spirit will take the shape of a beautiful woman, and if the person is a woman, then it appears as a handsome man. He also states that the spirit is always seen in the churchyard and that it is always in the evening, during the dark months of the year. The graveyard bride is said to be the ghost of a woman who was jilted at the altar and has been waiting for her man ever since. Only those who are about to die can see the phantom bride. The spirit is pleasant and charming, but it will get you to promise to meet again and whatever date the spirit chooses will be the date of the person's death.

Curran tells a story dating back to 1895 about a young man called John Torney, who came to a tragic end after meeting the graveyard bride. Although his family were originally from Co. Monaghan, he was living in the north of England and had returned home for a funeral. He was lingering after attending the burial and when he was about to leave, he saw a figure moving at a fast pace between gravestones, only stopping at the odd one to read the inscription.

As this female figure drew closer, he noticed how beautiful she was and if he hadn't just attended a funeral, he would have sworn he had been to a wedding because what stood before him was a beautiful bride dressed in white.

She had long dark hair, pale skin and blue eyes. Her beauty was apparent, but he could see that she was in deep despair. He asked her if she was looking for something and she explained to him that she had come to the graveyard to wait for a man, but because it was growing dark she was worried he wasn't going to show up and so she was forlorn.

She asked John if he would wait with her and he agreed, so they sat together on a stone and talked. She asked him many questions but did not give too much of herself away.

It was dark by now and it was obvious that the man the woman was waiting for had stood her up. John had enjoyed talking to her, so he asked her name. She said, 'I will not tell you my name now, but let's meet again, on this spot, one year from this evening and you will know everything about me.' And, before he could answer, the woman was gone. Up she got and she made her way back through the headstones until she disappeared completely.

John went back to his lodging and couldn't get the meeting out of his mind. It was quite unsettling and he had a bad feeling.

At breakfast the next morning, he told his host about the woman. His host went pale and quiet. John was worried and asked him why he was responding in such a way. He explained to him that the woman John had met was not a person but a ghost, the graveyard bride. She was notorious in the area for seeking out single men to marry. He said that it was a warning that he was not long for this world. He was advised to go and seek a priest to pray for his soul and that is what he did.

He heard similar stories from other people in the locality and so he feared the worst. He travelled back to his home in the north of England and tried to live life as normal. He was so frightened that he became depressed and didn't want to leave the house. He lost weight and couldn't think of anything other than the date the graveyard bride had set for him.

He knew he had to travel back to Monaghan on that exact date and meet his fate, so he thought that if he did so, he could persuade her to change her mind and maybe spare his life. This prospect gave him some hope.

When he arrived back in Ireland, he made his way to the graveyard where he had first met the woman. At first she was not there and then he saw something in the corner of his eye darting from grave to grave – it was the bride, his bride-to-be.

She threw her arms wide open and into them he fell.

John Torney was found in Errigal Truagh graveyard the next day. His body was found lying lifeless on a tombstone, with the most terrifying look of terror etched onto his face.

The inquest stated that he had died of a heart attack.

The church that was beside the graveyard is now a ruin and there have been no such stories in recent times, maybe because no one would dare to walk alone in the graveyard if they believed the tale that has been passed down in the parish for generations. But it is said that the place is haunted still and that if, on a dark evening, you should take a look at the graveyard, you can still catch a glimpse of a white gown darting from grave to grave.

In *Irish Ghosts*, Geddes and Grosset refer to William Carleton's poem about the graveyard. They state that Carleton became familiar with the story after speaking with locals and that afterwards he felt compelled to write about what he had been told:

> I have been shown the grave of a young person about eighteen years of age, who was said to have fallen victim to the phantom, and it is not more than ten weeks since a man in the same parish declared that he gave a promise and fatal kiss to the ghost and consequently looked upon himself as lost. He took a fever and was buried on the day appointed for the meeting, which was exactly a month from the time of contact with the spirit.

Friends of both men told Carleton that before the men passed away, they told the story of their meeting with the spirit in great detail. There was no variation between the two stories. Apparently, the spirit is sympathetic to the mourner, talks softly and tenderly and reassures the person that their deceased loved one is in a much happier place. The mourner becomes attracted to the spirit and forgets their grief. The attraction appears to be mutual and soon the two are holding hands and even kissing. When it is time to go, they arrange a time to meet again in the graveyard. As soon as the loving feelings wear off, the victim is filled with fear, but it is too late: the date is set, the date of their death.

William Carleton wrote a poem about the graveyard bride called 'Sir Turlough, or the Churchyard Bride'. When writing the poem, Carleton used the name 'Killeevy' instead of Errigal Truagh, which may simply have been because it fitted better with the rhyme.

Given the similarities between the churchyard bride and Bram Stoker's Dracula, it is thought that this folk tale may have been the inspiration for the famous vampire. It is a known fact that Bram Stoker visited Monaghan.

Carleton's use of the name 'Killeevy' may have been a reference to an ancient church and graveyard just over the border in Co. Armagh. The early convent of Killevy was founded towards the end of the fifth century by St Moninna, also known as Darerca or Bline, and part of it still stands today. It is known to be one of the earliest churches still in existence.

Sir Turlough, or the Churchyard Bride

THE BRIDE she bound her golden hair—
Killeevy, O Killeevy!
And her step was light as the breezy air
When it bends the morning flowers so fair,
By the bonnie green woods of Killeevy.

And O, but her eyes they danced so bright,
Killeevy, O Killeevy!
As she longed for the dawn of to-morrow's light,
Her bridal vows of love to plight,
By the bonnie green woods of Killeevy.

The bridegroom is come with youthful brow,
Killeevy, O Killeevy!
To receive from his Eva her virgin vow;
'Why tarries the bride of my bosom now?'
By the bonnie green woods of Killeevy.

A cry! A cry!—'t was her maidens spoke,
Killeevy, O Killeevy!
'Your bride is asleep—she has not awoke;
And the sleep she sleeps will be never broke,'
By the bonnie green woods of Killeevy.

Sir Turlough sank down with a heavy moan,
Killeevy, O Killeevy!
And his cheek became like the marble stone—

'O, the pulse of my heart is forever gone!'
By the bonnie green woods of Killeevy.

The keen is loud, it comes again,
Killeevy, O Killeevy!
And rises sad from the funeral train,
As in sorrow it winds along the plain,
By the bonnie green woods of Killeevy.

Now the grave is closed, and the mass is said,
Killeevy, O Killeevy!
And the bride she sleeps in her lonely bed,
The fairest corpse among the dead,
By the bonnie green woods of Killeevy.

The wreaths of virgin-white are laid,
Killeevy, O Killeevy!
By virgin hands, o'er the spotless maid;
And the flowers are strewn, but they soon will fade
By the bonnie green woods of Killeevy.

'O, go not yet—not yet away,
Killeevy, O Killeevy!
Let us feel that life is near our clay,'
The long-departed seem to say,
By the bonnie green woods of Killeevy.

But the tramp and the voices of life are gone,
Killeevy, O Killeevy!
And beneath each cold forgotten stone,
The mouldering dead sleep all alone,
By the bonnie green woods of Killeevy.

But who is he who lingereth yet?
Killeevy, O Killeevy!
The fresh green sod with his tears is wet,
And his heart in the bridal grave is set,
By the bonnie green woods of Killeevy.

O, who but Sir Turlough, the young and brave,
Killeevy, O Killeevy!
Should bend him o'er that bridal grave,
And to his death-bound Eva rave,
By the bonnie green woods of Killeevy.

'Weep not—weep not,' said a lady fair,
Killeevy, O Killeevy!
'Should youth and valor thus despair,
And pour their vows to the empty air?'
By the bonnie green woods of Killeevy.

There's charmed music upon her tongue,
Killeevy, O Killeevy!
Such beauty—bright, and warm, and young—
Was never seen the maids among,
By the bonnie green woods of Killeevy.

The charm is strong upon Turlough's eye,
Killeevy, O Killeevy!
His faithless tears are already dry,
And his yielding heart has ceased to sigh,
By the bonnie green woods of Killeevy.

'To thee,' the charmed chief replied,
Killeevy, O Killeevy!
'I pledge that love o'er my buried bride;
O, come, and in Turlough's hall abide,'
By the bonnie green woods of Killeevy.

Again the funeral voice came o'er
Killeevy, O Killeevy!
The passing breeze, as it wailed before,
And streams of mournful music bore,
By the bonnie green woods of Killeevy.

'If I to thy youthful heart am dear,
Killeevy, O Killeevy!

One month from hence thou wilt meet me here,
Where lay thy bridal Eva's bier,'
By the bonnie green woods of Killeevy.

He pressed her lips as the words were spoken,
Killeevy, O Killeevy!
And his banshee's wail—now far and broken—
Murmured 'Death,' as he gave the token,
By the bonnie green woods of Killeevy;

'Adieu! Adieu!' said this lady bright,
Killeevy, O Killeevy!
And she slowly passed like a thing of light,
Or a morning cloud, from Sir Turlough's sight,
By the bonnie green woods of Killeevy.

Now Sir Turlough has death in every vein,
Killeevy, O Killeevy!
And there's fear and grief o'er his wide domain,
And gold for those who will calm his brain,
By the bonnie green woods of Killeevy.

The leech has failed, and the hoary priest,
Killeevy, O Killeevy!
With pious shrift his soul released,
And the smoke is high of his funeral feast,
By the bonnie green woods of Killeevy.

The shanachies now are assembled all,
Killeevy, O Killeevy!
And the songs of praise, in Sir Turlough's hall,
To the sorrowing harp's dark music fall,
By the bonnie green woods of Killeevy.

And there is trophy, banner, and plume,
Killeevy, O Killeevy!
And the pomp of death, with its darkest gloom,
O'ershadows the Irish chieftain's tomb,
By the bonnie green woods of Killeevy.

The month is closed, and Green Truagha's pride,
Killeevy, O Killeevy!
Is married to death—and, side by side,
He slumbers now with his churchyard bride,
By the bonnie green woods of Killeevy.

24

SUPERSTITIONS AND
TALES FROM THE
NATIONAL FOLKLORE
COLLECTION

*These stories and pieces about superstition are recorded in the National
Folklore Collection, held at the Newman Building at UCD. The
collection consists of folklore material collected by 11–14-year-old
primary school students during 1937–38, and is separated in volumes
by school, parish, townland and county, so that specific areas may be
explored. They are all retold by children and have all the innocence
and enthusiasm of a child's imagination combined with the oral tradition that was still very much alive at the time.*

*In 1937, in collaboration with the Department of Education and
the Irish National Teachers Organisation, this wonderful scheme was
initiated to encourage schoolchildren to collect folklore and local history
from their areas. Over a period of eighteen months some 100,000
children in over 5,000 National Schools in twenty-six counties in the
Republic of Ireland took part. They were asked to look at all different
areas, including folklore. So there were myths, legends, songs, poems,
riddles, cures, games, crafts and a whole plethora of many other traditions and pastimes.*

*Most of the work was gathered by the children from their parents
and grandparents, other family members and older neighbours. It is
a truly remarkable collection of magnificent original material and*

*a real treasure trove for anyone interested in folklore and folk tradi-
tions. These are stories collected by children in Co. Monghan during
the 1930s. The text is exactly as written or transcribed.*

FIRST DAY OF MAY

There was a lot of superstitions in Ireland long ago and there are
many that have survived until the present day. The first day of May
is one day that had a lot of superstitions associated with it. It was
thought that witches went about on that day, generally in the shape
of a hare that would take the milk from a cow at every house the
witches visited.

On 1 May, country people would not borrow or lend anything.
Anybody with a spring well on their own land would try to be the
first at it on that morning.

A man was on his way to the Monaghan market once when he
met two men on the road. He said to himself that these men were
unlucky and that it would be better to turn back home. So this is
what he did.

A lot of these old saying are bad.

Bragan (p. 135)

'COMPOSITION OLD ROADS' (19 OCTOBER 1938)

I hear the oldest road in our district is the one through Drumfurrer.
It was an old bog pass at one time and it went straight from
Glenmore to Augher and Clogher. It was older than the broad road
which is used now instead of the Drumfurrer one on the Glen road
as we call it. There is a bridge on it which was built sixty years ago
across a little river running from Killabern Lough. A good many
people are afraid to go past it at a late hour of the night as the people
say there is a ghost at it. From the time of the famine in 1847, old
people say there was a hungry man coming along the road and the
only thing he could get was beans and he ate too much and died at
this bridge before it was built.

Since then people call it 'Planksty'. As the same man that died was of that name. It must be a very old road because William Carleton the famous writer mentioned it in his story writing.

He used to travel this road going from Clogher where he was born, to friends of his in Deragola, called McCarrons. He mentioned in some part of a story about the 'Moonlight Walk' on Drumfurrer road. Carleton's Country.

Mary B. Hackett
Tavnacrinn
Co. Tyrone

Bragan (p. 134)

Loch Diarmada

Norah Cooney, Corcreagh NS, collected this story from Bridie Lynch, Lisnadara, Parish of Aughnamullan, Co. Monaghan.

This is about a lake on Bridie Lynch's farm. Loch Diarmada was once an enchanted lake. Long ago there was an old man living in a little cave in the spelic (a large stone near the lake). This cave is still to be seen. The man was a shoemaker and after his death the lake appeared.

Every seven years there used to come wild horses out of the lake and feed on the grass and then go back again. Once her grandfather let two horses out to drink at a pond near the lake. In about half-an-hour, he went to take them home, but when he was approaching them, he heard something like the sound of neighing in the lake and then he saw the two horses running towards it. He ran after them but they jumped into the lake and were gone.

He came back again feeling that his horses were gone, but when he came back to the pond his two horses were feeding alongside of it. He went up to them and brought them home. It was the wild horses he was following.

School: Cor Críochach
Location: Corcreeghagh, Co.
Monaghan
Teacher: Ss Ó Muireadhaigh

Bragan (p. 276)

THE WATER BULL OF DRUM LOCH

My father says that there is a water bull in Drum Loch in the townland of Cortober. This bull was about the size of a yearling calf. It lived in the part of the lake below Dr Moor's house. It used to destroy and scatter his hay at night. Every morning he used to get up to find out what was destroying his hay. One morning he got up very early and went out to see. When he went out he saw a bull running away into the lake. Next morning he got up earlier and brought a gun with him. He fired a shot at it but missed it. The bull was never seen out of the lake again.

Collected by May Molloy
School: Killyfargy
Location: Killyfargy, Co. Monaghan
Teacher: B. Ó Mórdha
(p. 32)

THE WATER-HORSES

Once upon a time there was a man coming home from his ceilidh and he had to pass by Drumcor Lough which lies a couple of miles from Redhills between Cavan and Monaghan. As he was passing by he saw two water-horses drinking out of the Lough. He went over to them but they went back into the Lough and began to swim. Then they looked like two big eels.

Collected by Brigid Brides
School: Killyfargy
Location: Killyfargy, Co. Monaghan
Teacher: B. Ó Mórdha
(p. 33)

THE WORM DITCH

The Worm Ditch runs through this parish of Currin Co. Monaghan. The remains of it can still be seen in the townland of Cornapast or Laurelhill. Much of it was formerly dug away here. Trace of it can be seen in Annaghan[?] and in Knocks. It is best preserved in Crussin and Aghareagh. Here it runs through a gap in the hills and then up the side of Aghareagh hills in direction of Murdock's cross near Drum. The names of some of the townlands derive from it (eg Cornaposte (cor-na-péiste) Mullanample, etc.) In Crussin and Aghareagh it is a huge double dyke about twenty feet across and twelve feet deep. There are little or no stories connected with it. The people simply say that it divided Ireland in two. I haven't come across any stories so far about the 'peist' from which it took its name or even about the black pig which is sometimes associated with it. It was in some townlands looked on with a kind of superstitious dread; this helped its preservation. In other parts of the parish it has been levelled. Old people say that good luck didn't follow the levellers. This 'Worm Ditch' is the greatest historical landmark in the parish; indeed one of the greatest in Ulster.

Collected by Séamus P. Ó Mórdha
Location: Killyfargy, Co. Monaghan
Teacher: B. Ó Mórdha
(p. 33–4)

A BANSHEE STORY

Nearly forty years ago, my grandmother, then a young woman, lived in Armagh. Her parents lived in Cookstown, County Tyrone. One evening at dusk, about seven o'clock, she heard a strange cry in the back-yard. On going to the back-door she saw a little woman crossing the yard, crying as she vanished. On the following morning, she got a telegram that her mother was dead. It was said then that the Banshee followed her family.

Collected by: Miss Dympna Magee
School: Tulach Chromán
Location: Tullycroman, Co. Monaghan
Teacher: Mrs. Brennan

THE THING ON THE BRIDGE

This following story was collected by a student from the same school that Patrick Kavanagh attended as a child.

One night as Michael __ was coming from his ceilidh across Ednamo Bridge, near Inniskeen with a pack of cards in his pocket. He was stopped by something which he could not recognise as a man or a beast. He soon took off his coat to give fight but then 'the thing' disappeared. But when Michael looked again it re-appeared. It moved with him over and back and Michael got weak, finding beads of perspiration standing out all over him and every hair seemed to stand like fibre on his head.

He got strength to put his hand into his pocket where he had the cards. And as soon as he threw them out, he got away without any trouble.

Collected by A. Nic Aonguis
School: Céad na Mínseach
Location: Kednaminsha, Inniskeen, Co. Monaghan
Teacher: M. Nic Aodha
(p. 121)

25

MONAGHAN FOLK SONGS

Here is a collection of old Monaghan folk songs, which capture the essence of the county and also the mystery of its landscape and people.

In 1607, Patrick McKenna was given 250 acres of the Barony of Truagh in north County Monaghan by the Lord Chief Deputy of Ireland. It was from here that Major John McKenna 'rode at noon' to join Owen Roe O'Neill. At the Battle of Drumbanagher, he was killed in battle and became the first casualty of the Williamite Wars.

The Shady Woods of Truagh

From out the shady woods of Truagh, MacKenna rides at noon.
The sun shines brightly, not a cloud darkens the skys of June;
No eye has he for nature's charms, they don't distract his brain
As through the flowery vales he takes his way and never draws the
    reins.

Until before him loom the towers of Glaslough Castle's Hold,
Which holds a treasure in its walls more dear to him than gold,
For in it dwells his own true love, the dark-eyed young Maureen
Whom he hopes that God will bless his home in the woods of
    Truagh so green.

'I have come to look upon you, love, for it's soon that I must go
With my brave Truagh men to Benburb, there to defend Owen
    Roe.
I have come to look upon you, Love, and hear your answer sweet
For I might in the battle fall and we might never meet.'

'Go forth, my love, my blessings go and smite the Saxon horde
And when you return I'll be your bride without another word.'
Within fond embrace, they bid adieu as the evening sun went down
Behind yon western wooded hill that overlooks Glaslough town.

MacKenna lightly mounts his steed at the twilight of the eve
And he heads her over Dasa Hill and Truagh's green shady lee.
That night he leads his gallant men o'er the dark hills of Tyrone
To meet the army of the North at Benburb on their own.

Right well O'Neill was glad to see those gallant mountaineers
Who kept the Saxon wolves at bay round ancient Truagh for years.
Full well they fought on Benburb's plains as England's flag went
    down
And few that night escaped them toward Carrickfergus town.

The autumn's winds being in the air and berries ripe and red,
MacKenna and his lovely bride in Glaslough church were wed
And never in her father's thoughts a fairer bride was seen
Than McMahon's only daughter, the dark-eyed young Maureen.

The Green Woods of Truagh

In the green woods of Truagh we met without fear,
Your kiss on my lips, and your voice in my ear,
Your tender arms about me, and your eyes glad and clear –
Ochón, the Green Woods of Truagh!

In the green woods of Truagh the days go on wings,
On every brown branch a gladsome bird sings
And the fragrant amber blossom of the honey-suckle swings –
Ochón, the Green Woods of Truagh!

In the green woods of Truagh the bracken stands high,
And wells of spring-water in deep hollows lie,
And the red deer is browsing in the cool shadows nigh –
Ochón, the Green Woods of Truagh!

In the green woods of Truagh no sorrow dared stay,
The lark called me early at dawn o' the day,
And o'er my sleep at night pleasant dreams used to play –
Ochón, the Green Woods of Truagh!

In the green woods of Truagh you wait till I come;
I left home and you for the stranger's far home,
To bring a hoard of yellow gold across the grey foam –
Ochón, the Green Woods of Truagh!

In the green woods of Truagh, if God hears my prayer,
I shall reach you, O true love, my empty hands there,
For little of the yellow gold has fallen to my share –
Ochón, the Green Woods of Truagh!

In the green woods of Truagh, your heart on my own,
And your bright hair in ringlets across my cheek blown;
Now where in all the wide, wide world, could greater bliss be known?
Ochón, the Green Woods of Truagh!

Written by Ethna Carbery (Mrs Seumus MacManus, Anna Johnston, 1866–1902)

The Road to Ballybay

'Is this the road to Ballybay?'
Says I to Miss Magee;
'You're leaving it behind you,'
Says Mary Anne to me.

So I turned and walked beside her
And 'tis only fair to say
It was very pleasant walking
On the road to Ballybay.

Ballybay, Ballybay,
'twas a dark and wintery day
But the sun was surely shining
On the road to Ballybay.

'Is this the road to fame and wealth?'
Says I to Miss Magee;
'You've got the brains, you've got the health,'
Says Mary Anne to me.

'But still I want a comrade
To praise me and to blame
And keep me from the traps that's laid
Upon the road to fame.'

Ballybay, Ballybay,
No man could go astray
With a guide like her beside him
On the road to Ballybay.

'Is this the road to paradise?'
Says I to Miss Magee;
'I'm thinking that it might be,'
Says Mary Anne to me.

I saw the love light leaping
In a pair of roguish eyes
And I knew we two were stepping
On the road to paradise.

Ballybay, Ballybay,
The birds are far away
But our hearts they sang together
On the road to Ballybay.

Percy French (1 May 1854–24 January 1920)

Paddy at the Theatre

From the county of Monaghan lately I came.
I'm a tinker by trade, Laeey Dooly's my name.
My cousin Tim Murphy, I met yesterday;
Says he, Mr Dooly, you'll come to a play?
Derry down down down, Derry down.

Is it the play that you mean? Are you sure that you're right?
They're treating the town to Pizzaro tonight,
But the treat as he called it, and the one that I mean
Bad luck to his treat, it cost me all my tin.
Derry down down down, Derry down.

The green curtain drew up and a lady I spied
When a man came to kiss her, she scornfully cried,
Get out you big blackguard, I'll bother your jig,
When in comes Pizzaro with a grunt like a pig
Derry down down down, Derry down.

In the days of ould Goury, a long time ago,
The Spaniards claimed war 'gainst Peru, you know,
They claimed its cash, its jewels and keys
When a boy they called Rowler says: No, if you please.
Derry down down down, Derry down.

Then Rowler came in, like a day-star appeared
He made a long speech and the sojers all cheered
Says he, 'Beat well the Spaniards, and do the neat thing
And then boys, stand up for your country and king.'
Derry down down down, Derry down.

Then Mr. Murphy Alonzo somehow went to jail;
He got out by a back door without giving bail.
While Rowler was jumping o'er bridges and greens,
He was shot by some blackguard behind the big screens
Derry down down down, Derry down.

Then Rowler came forward, and with him a child,
Looking all for the world like a man that was wild.
'Here's your gossoon, dear Cora, it's my own blood that's spilt
In defence of your child, blood an' hounds, I'm kilt.'
Derry down down down, Derry down.

Then Alonzo and Pizzaro had a terrible fight;
Pizzaro got killed, that seemed perfectly right
For the audience came down with a shower of applause.
They were all enlisted in the Peruvian's cause.
Derry down down down, Derry down.

Then Alonzo came forward and handsomely bowed
Saying: Ladies and gentlemen, meaning the crowd
By your kind permission, to-morrow, then
We'll murder Pizzaro all over again.
Derry down down down, Derry down.

26

FAIRY STORIES

Whilst travelling around Co. Monaghan, I met many people and these people told me all sorts of wonderful stories about the fairy folk and what they get up to. As a storyteller, I am fascinated by the Good Folk, which they are better known as in Ireland. So it was a real joy to be given so many of their tales. I was amazed at the sheer wealth and quality of fairy stories that I came across and I am delighted to be able to include them in this collection of folk tales.

A HILL IN SHEETRIM

In a part of Monaghan known as Mullyerra, there lived a man named James McAree. Now, James had a cow that he was very proud of and every day he would go and milk the cow. But then something very strange happened. Well, one day like any other, he went to perform his milking duties and, lo and behold, the cow was already milked and the pail was full to the brim.

So early one evening, auld Mrs McAree went out early to get the cow and was shocked to see two wee men milking the cow. When she got closer, she realised they were fairy folk, those funny-looking craturs with long pointy noses and ears to boot, no more than a couple of feet tall.

But as soon as they saw her, they ran as fast as the wind, up the next hill into Sheetrim.

No one knows if these fairies were ever seen again but there were sightings of members of the Good Folk in Co. Monaghan and here are a few that were recorded.

Skeveran Fort

There was an auld woman called Mary Martin, who, for some strange reason, decided to spend one night alone in Skeveran Fort, near Smithsborough. When she awoke, she saw a mare and a foal standing beside her and at their feet was a pile of the most beautiful rosy apples that you have ever seen.

The horses nudged the apples, as if to encourage the woman to take them. Well, she was very hungry and wasted no time collecting them into her apron. As soon as she looked up, the horses were gone, with not a sign nor a trace of them to be seen, and so she decided to head home.

On her way back, she met another woman on the road and kindly offered her a few of the lovely apples, telling her the strange tale of how she had acquired them. But as soon as she went to give the other woman some of the strange fruit, she was shocked to see that her apron was full of '*maothlach*', or horse manure.

It was said that you should never try to give away a fairy gift …

Sí Gaoithe

One night, there was a man coming home from a ceilidh in Knockatallon. Before he had gone far, he found himself amongst a mighty gathering of people. Now, what was even more peculiar about all of this was the fact that they all knew his name and addressed him every time they spoke to him.

Well now, they took him to a fine big castle and there they gave him all sorts of magnificent food and drink. But the man refused to eat or drink any of it for he knew that he was in the company of the fairy folk, and his mother had warned him when he was a child never to partake of any food or drink offered to you by the fairy folk, for if you did you would be under their spell and would remain their slave for all eternity.

So then they took him to a place called Ervy in Co. Fermanagh and no one knows what went on there. He was found the next morning lying in the glen, but there was no sign of the fairies.

When the people went to see if the man was all right and what he was doing there, he disappeared right in front of their eyes and found himself safe and sound at home again.

Well, everything was fine until exactly a year later, when the same man was on his way home from Roslea.

Just as he was about to reach his house, he heard and felt the '*sí gaoithe*', or the fairy wind, rising up about him. And then the inevitable happened: he was whipped up by the wind and was about to be whisked off by the fairies again when he called out with all his might. Luckily for him, some of his neighbours were close by and saw to their horror and bewilderment what was happening to their friend.

They all ran after him and managed to overtake him at Drummons, where they caught him and threw him into a bog hole. The fairy wind shrieked and moaned as it moved off into the distance. After that, the man was never bothered by the fairies again and he always made sure to keep some sort of iron or steel on his person to protect himself from their enchantments, because the fairies do not like iron or steel. Apparently a little steel crucifix did the job nicely.

THE CHANGELING OF DRUMCOO

There was once a husband and wife, called the Heaghneys, who lived in the townland of Drumcoo (Foster) in Co. Monaghan.

Now, they had always wanted a child and they had tried for a long time to have one until eventually they were blessed with a wee child of their own.

In those days, a child was always kept in a cradle and as a precaution an iron tongs was placed above the cradle to protect the child from the fairies. The fairy folk do not like iron or steel, which render their enchantments powerless.

Well, one day Mrs Heaghney was outside milking the cow, but hadn't she forgotten to put the tongs across the cradle. When she went back inside the house, to her horror she saw that there was a strange, monstrous-looking creature in the cradle, snarling up at

her. She knew fine rightly that this was not her own wee child but a changeling left behind by the fairies.

She went and got her husband and both of them were very upset and they did not know what to do. They were told that there was a wee man who lived in the townland of Knocknagrave in the parish of Trough, Co. Monagahan, who had experience of getting stolen children back from the fairies. So they went to see him and he told them what to do. Well, they were not too happy with what they heard and were a bit reluctant at first but they were told that if they did not get rid of the changeling, life would be very difficult for them.

So they went home and did as they were told: they built a great big turf fire in the fireplace and put the cradle with the changeling in it right next the fire itself. As the fire grew hotter and hotter, it became too hot to even be in the wee house, so they went outside. Now, as they stood outside they could hear the cries of the child inside the house. Poor Mrs Heaghney wanted to relent and go inside for the child, but Mr Heaghney told her not to and that she must remember that it was not their child in there but a changeling.

Well, after a while, they heard a terrible scream and a loud bang and above them they saw the changeling fly out the chimney and disappear into the sky.

They ran back inside the house and there they found their own child, safe and well. They took it outside of the house as it was still ferociously hot and they swore that they would never leave the wee one alone again without safeguarding it from the fairy folk.

INISKEEN'S ON FIRE

This wee story about 'a changeling' was originally told by a lady called Ellen Cutler from Co. Fermanagh and was collected by the folklorist Henry Glassie in his book Irish Folk Tales *(1985).*

Iniskeen means 'peaceful island'. It is a small village and parish in south Monaghan, close to the Co. Louth and south Armagh borders. It is probably most famous for being the home of the great poet and writer Patrick Kavanagh, who is buried at Iniskeen cemetery. But according to this wee tale, Inniskeen was at one time the home of the wee folk or the fairies ... This story is written as it was collected.

FAIRY STORIES   171

There was a woman and she had a wee baby boy in a cradle. In them days, there was no such thing as a pram. So, this boy came in and the child was taken out of the cradle and this 'funny boy' got into it. The child was never seen and the funny boy was in the cradle all the time.

And a man come in, a neighbour man come in, and he, the boy in the cradle, says, 'Gimme a light for me pipe!' 'Gimme a coal there outta the fire.'

So the boyo got the coal and he smoked.

And then there was another man going to a blacksmith. He was going to get a loy fixed. (A loy was an early Irish spade with a long heavy handle made from the ash plant, a narrow steel plate on the face and a single footrest. The word loy comes from the Irish word '*láí*', which means spade. It was used for manual ploughing prior to and during the Great Famine of Ireland, 1845–1852.) It wasn't a spade now; it was a loy. So, the man was going away to get the loy fixed with the blacksmith. He looked into the cradle and he knew that it was no child.

He knew it was no baby. And the boy in the cradle put up his head and says, 'Would you give me a light for me pipe!' So the man that went in, he went out again onto the street, and he let a big curse out of him: 'Inniskeen's on fire! Inniskeen's on fire! Inniskeen's on fire!'

So the boyo got up and hopped out of the cradle and was away and he was never seen again.

He was frightened, you see, when he heard about the fire in Inniskeen.

That's where they lived, you see. I often heard me husband telling it. The man says, 'Inniskeen's on fire!', so he disappeared. I often heard him telling me that.

BOULD BILLIE McKENNA AND THE FAIRY FOLK

I am sure most of us know, or at least knew, someone who seemed to know a lot about the fairies and their carry-on about the place. Well, one of these characters was a fella called Billie McKenna from the town of Monaghan. He seemed to have a real affinity with the wee folk and a huge respect for them. The following is the story of one of his adventures with the wee folk.

One bright moonlit night, Billie McKenna was returning home at a steady and easy pace. It was a beautiful night and Billie was enjoying the walk, charmed by the whistling wind and the silvery glow from the moon that made everything about him shimmer like the surface of a still lake.

But this was all to change when he came to Davidson's meadow. He had passed this meadow many times before and it was never the sort of thing that really caught his attention, but on this night, he was stopped in his tracks for the meadow was full of men on horseback, all of them very well dressed and smaller than normal men.

One of them trotted over to poor Billie, who was quite frightened at this stage, and the funny wee cratur looked down at Billie from his magnificent black steed and asked if he would like to go for a ride with them. What really put the fear into Billie was the fact that the wee man knew his full name and addressed him as if he had been expecting him.

Well, Billie was no fool and he knew straight away that he was in the company of the good folk and to be rude or impolite to them on a moonlit night such as this would be very foolish – indeed, even fatal. So, he told the wee man that he would love to go for a ride with them, but it was very late in the night and unfortunately he had no horse anyway.

The wee man pointed down at a big clump of ragweed growing in the ditch beside where Billie stood.

'Pull that ragweed growing beside you in the ditch,' commanded the wee man.

Well, Billie did as he was told and pulled the ragweed from the ditch, and as soon as he did he found himself straddled across the back of a beautiful white calf.

'Hi for Navan Fort!' cried out the wee man on the black horse.

Now, Navan Fort, for anyone who may not know, is an ancient Celtic fort in Co. Armagh which was owned by Conchobar Mac Nessa, the High King of Ulster.

Well now, Billie just went along with what the men did and cried out himself, 'Hi! For Navan Fort!'

So off they went to Navan Fort in County Armagh, Billie and the troop of fairy horsemen galloping across hills, ditches, lakes, rivers and orchards at speeds that would make your head spin. Billie held on to the silk reins that hung from a golden bit in the calf's mouth. The wee animal flew through the air and Billie was never so excited in all his life, watching the moonlit countryside fly past below him and seeing the world in a way that he had never thought possible.

Billie was totally ecstatic and he cried out, 'Holy God, this is powerful altogether!'

At that point, the leader rode up beside him and looked at him with a very angry expression indeed. Billie could not understand what he had done wrong at all.

Then the leader said to him in a loud and agitated voice, 'Don't mention God's name in any of our dealings this night!'

'All right, your honour,' replied Billie apologetically.

The fairy man nodded his head and said, 'Let that be the end of it and hi for Navan Fort!'

So on they galloped and cleared every hedge, ditch and river they came across. Billie was very pleased with his wee calf and impressed by how well it jumped and flew across the land.

He shouted out with great admiration for his steed, 'That I never be damned but you are a well-leaped calf!'

The going was furious and Billie was afraid he might fall off, so he leant into the beast as it flew along like a beautiful bird.

As they rode along, the cold wind and the chilling air made Billie sneeze.

He blurted out, 'God bless me!'

With that, the fairy leader came up alongside Billie. He had a rush in his hand, which he used to whip the calf on its rump, making it give a big buck-leap and the next thing Billie found himself clinging to a bunch of rushes on the edge of a bog hole in Killyneill bog, 4 miles from Carickavon.

Well, Billie told that story every time anyone ever asked why he never owned or rode a horse.

Tales of Johnny McKenna and the Good Folk

Now, I came across quite a few stories about a Johnny McKenna, but there are so many McKennas in Monaghan that it could be the same man in all the stories or a different man with the same name each time.

Anyway, here we go. I hope you enjoy these stories of Johnny McKenna and the fairies.

In the townland of Drumgaghan in Co. Monaghan, there once lived a man called Johnny McKenna, who was a great fiddler. One winter's night at around eight o'clock, he was sitting comfortably by the fire in his own house, when all of a sudden there was a knock at the door. Now, 'twas strange as the knock came from quite low down on the door, like it was a small child knocking. Johnny thought this was odd and wondered what on earth a wee child was doing out at this time on a dark, cold winter night and what on earth the child was doing knocking on his door.

Well, Johnny got up and answered the door and to his great surprise he saw a wee man standing there. Now, Johnny had never seen this wee man before in his life, but the wee man knew Johnny.

'Hello John!' says the wee man, with all the familiarity of a close friend. 'I hear that you're a great fiddler, John.'

Johnny replied, 'Well, I'm not too bad, I suppose.'

With that, the wee man got all excited and piped up, 'Well, can ya play me a few tunes then, John?'

Johnny was very taken aback by all of this for it was most peculiar and very strange indeed, but Johnny was no fool and he knew fine rightly that the wee man was not flesh and blood like you and I. He knew that this wee cratur was one of the Good Folk, or the fairy folk, and he knew it was very wise to be as pleasant with them as possible for it always paid off to be polite to them, especially if they turn up unannounced at night!

So Johnny took down his fiddle and he began to play late into the night and the wee man danced around the place, laughing and play-acting like a wee boy. Then, at the stroke of midnight, the wee man stopped dancing and announced in a loud voice, 'I must go now! It's getting late, Johnny. Can you leave your hat on the floor and please don't look out the door after me when I leave? Just close the door once I am gone.'

Well, Johnny opened the door and let him away into the night. Some folk say that Johnny peeped out after him and he saw nothing at all and when he lifted his hat there was a piece of clay under it and others say that Johnny did exactly as he was told and closed the door after the wee man and when he looked under the hat he found a wee pile of gold coins.

THE FAIRY PIPE

Now, there was a Johnny McKenna who lived in the townland of Killybrone in Clara, Co. Monaghan and he was out ploughing his field one fine spring day. It was getting towards evening and his two horses were starting to get very tired indeed. So he thought it was time to give himself and his two beasts of burden a well-deserved rest. He sat down on a large flat stone at the top of the field and he proceeded to take out his pipe and light it up. He loved a wee 'drag' or 'draw' on his pipe every now and again. Sure, it was altogether very common at the time for the country farmers to smoke a pipe.

Now, when he had rested himself and his horses and satisfied himself with a few relaxing puffs on his pipe, he placed the pipe on the large flat stone and he continued with his ploughing until it got dark and it was really time to call it a day. Well, Johnny was as good a man as he was hard-working and he took the horses home and made sure they were well fed and watered. He groomed them and gave them fresh bedding. When he was finished with the horses, he washed his hands in the wee stream in front of the house and went inside to have his supper. When he had finished eating, he reached into his pocket to get his pipe, but it was 'gone'. Well, he remembered leaving it on the big flat stone at the top of the field, so off he went to get it back. But when he got there, it was nowhere to be seen at all.

He searched everywhere, but there was no sign of it at all. The next day, he went, thinking that with the light, he would have better luck finding it, but there was nothing there at all. He thought this was very strange and then it was explained to him that the large flat stone at the top of the field was part of a fairy fort, so there must have been a fairy path running through his field. All of his ploughing had broken up the path and the fairies would have been very annoyed about this. So taking his pipe was a small sign of their annoyance. Luckily for Johnny, he was a good and a kind man, so the fairies went easy on him and about two years afterwards he found his pipe on top of the flat stone, exactly where he had left it. There was even a bit of tobacco in it too.

JOHNNY MCKENNA AND THE KING OF THE FAIRIES

Tydavnet, Co. Monaghan, was always well known for its 'dealin' men' or 'wide boys' – in other words, men that knew how to buy and sell everything from cattle, sheep and horses and always get a good price.

Now, Johnny McKenna was one of these dealin' men. He was one of the best and he claimed only ever to work with the best of stock and breed. But he would also know how to dabble with lesser stock to cater for the less affluent clients, for a sale was a sale after all and Johnny would travel to all the fairs and marts in Monaghan and the surrounding counties to get what he was looking for.

Well, it so happened that the parish priest was looking for a new pony as this was a long time ago, before we had motor cars or buses and maybe even trains. So when Johnny heard about this, he wasted no time at all – he set out on foot for the Fintona fair in Co. Tyrone.

When the bould Johnny got to the fair in Fintona, all the good stock had gone and there was nothing that caught his eye, so he decided to cut his losses and head away for home again. On the way back, he met a wee man who told him of a great shortcut over the mountain. Now, anyone who knows anything about wee men and shortcuts will tell you to avoid such advice and to stick to the road that you know yourself.

The wee man told him that if he took this shortcut, it would save him 8 or 9 miles on his journey. Now, anyone who knows anything about walking long distances will agree that this is a massive saving indeed. Well, he decided to take the shortcut and it was not long before he found himself lost. There he was, gone astray over the mountain, not knowing if he was coming or going.

Well now, poor Johnny must have been wandering along the lonely, dark and winding mountain roads for over half the night when all of a sudden he saw a light in the distance. He was relieved to see this beacon of hope and he wasted no time making his way towards it.

As he got closer to the light, he realised that it was coming from a wee cottage, thatched with heather and no more than about 4 feet high. It was a strange-looking little building, but Johnny was glad to be outside of it and not wandering aimlessly around the mountain. Johnny knocked on the wee half-door and an old woman answered by opening the door and poking her wizened face out at him.

'Who are ye?' asked the old woman in a shrill voice.

Johnny answered by stating, 'I am a poor man who is off his path.'

'Come in,' says the auld one.

Well, Johnny stooped down and nearly had to crawl into the house. He got the fright of his life for right before him, lying on the floor of the old shack, was a dead sheep. Now, Johnny gasped and let out a bit of a shout.

'Hould your whist and speak easy!' growled the old woman, then she looked at him and went on to explain her anxiety. 'I am afraid that the men will hear and they might come in. They are a bad lot and the work they do I don't like it one bit: they are stealing sheep and killing them!' She then pointed towards the back of the house and said, 'Now, go down to the room there. There's a bed there where you can rest yourself.'

Well, poor Johnny made his way down the hall to the room and he was bewildered at how big the house was inside for outside it was nothing more than a tiny hovel. Johnny opened the door to the room and was surprised to find that he was in a fine big room with a very large and comfortable bed in it. He lay down and rested his weary bones on the soft feathered mattress.

Now, he was not long in the bed when he heard a loud knock on the front door. He sat up and heard the old woman say, 'Speak easy, for there is a man down in the room and he is trying to get a bit of rest.'

Johnny was terrified for he knew she was talking to the terrible sheep-stealers. He knew such men would not be happy to think that there was a stranger in the house who knew of their dealings and he knew that they would make sure he would not tell anyone of their existence.

Well, Johnny's fears were confirmed for he heard a gruff male voice replying, 'He won't be long in it!'

Johnny heard the man sharpening a knife, so he jumped up out of the bed and jumped out an open window. He was only out the window when three men came down to the room. When they saw him outside, they dived out the window like wild dogs after him. As he ran for his life, Johnny eventually came to a big river and got in under the banks. When the men reached the river they searched up and down, poking the riverbanks with knives and sticks and whooping and howling like wolves.

Then Johnny heard one of them say, 'Hey, didn't I tell you, the thief is away with the flood.'

Johnny stayed under the riverbank for over two long hours until there came a wee man about 2 feet high. He stood on the opposite bank, looked at Johnny with great puzzlement and called out, 'Well now, what happened you?'

'I have been out all night and and what a terrible night it has been – I was nearly murdered!' Johnny cried out.

Then the moonlight shone on the river, revealing a footstick, which is a makeshift bridge consisting of a log thrown across the river. The wee man crossed the footstick to where Johnny was and took him back over to his side. He asked Johnny if he was hungry and Johnny replied that he was starving, so the wee man produced a loaf of wheaten bread and a jug of fresh buttermilk. Johnny was very grateful and consumed them with great haste and appreciation. The food made him feel powerful, giving him the strength of two men.

The wee man then produced a whistle, which he blew with great ferocity. As soon as he did, two magnificent horses (the likes of which Johnny had never seen in all his years as a 'dealin' man'), wearing fine saddles and bridles, appeared out of nowhere. The wee man mounted one of these beasts and then he told Johnny to get on the other, which he did.

'Watch yourself now!' says the wee man. 'For we have very rough and dangerous roads before us.'

Well, the horses galloped like the wind for a couple of hours until Johnny found himself in the Bog of Allen. The atmosphere was strange and haunting. Although he knew that the horses were walking on the soft peat of the bog, their hooves clattered as though they were trotting along on a hard and stony road and above his head flew flocks of wild geese in their thousands – the sky was black with them, like swarms of giant midges.

It seemed like they were trotting and galloping through the haunted bog for an awful long time before they eventually came out of it and Johnny saw before him a mighty plain covered in thick snow. But before he had a chance to admire this beautiful sight, he found himself galloping across a wide and magnificent lough. The horses galloped across it as if it were a broad highway. After they had crossed the lough, they soon reached a dark and mysterious underground tunnel. They entered the tunnel, which was like entering the mouth of a giant worm – it twisted and turned deep down into the earth. They were in total darkness the whole time. They trotted along in silence for a very long time indeed, until they saw a great light in the distance.

Now, Johnny and the wee man arrived at a great gated entrance adorned with burning lamps. The gates were huge and made from a dark wood decorated with magnificent carvings. The gates opened before them and the two men trotted inside. They were greeted by two rows of over a million men, all about 2 feet tall and dressed in the richest of finery. These strange men took them into the grandest hall that Johnny had ever seen. It was as if someone had put a roof on the world and decorated it with all the jewels of nature. In this magical hall, there were tables covered with every sort of food and drink you could imagine and more besides.

Johnny was treated like royalty. He was told to take a seat, make himself comfortable and eat and drink as much as he liked. He was also told to take his time and to enjoy the feast, 'For the man who made time, made plenty of it!'

Forty fiddlers appeared out of nowhere and started playing mighty jigs and reels. There was wild dancing and singing in the great hall. Then the wee man whom he had travelled with put up his hand and all the dancing and music stopped right then and there.

The wee man pointed at poor Johnny, who was quite caught off guard as only a second ago he had been dancing and singing to his heart's content.

The wee man then shouted in al oud and shrill voice, 'Look now! There is the man who needs to take a rest!'

With that, Johnny was taken away by a group of wee men, who were very strong, considering their small stature and size. He was taken to a lovely bedroom, which was a great relief to Johnny for he was sure he was going to be thrown into a dungeon or some class of deep, dark hole in the ground.

Well now, there was a fire burning in a big ornate fireplace in this room. The fuel for the fire was neither turf, wood nor coal – Johnny could not tell what it was at all, but there was a mighty heat from it that warmed the whole house like toast and as soon as Johnny hit the bed, he was fast asleep like a wee baby.

When Johnny awoke, daylight was streaming in like rays of a rainbow through the beautiful stained-glass windows that adorned the great walls of the magnificent room. He sat up in the giant four-poster bed and saw before him a huge wooden table laden with fabulous food and drink of every sort and kind. He got himself dressed and was about to sit down to his majestic breakfast when the great door of his room opened and the wee man arrived in, all smiles.

He said to Johnny, 'You will not get away until you have seen all about this place.'

So after Johnny had eaten and drank his fill, the wee man took him on a grand tour. It looked like a palace and covered as much as two, if not three, acres of land. Johnny had never seen the likes of it in all his days. It was truly breathtaking and beautiful beyond description.

Well, it was time for Johnny to go home and he thanked his wee friend ever so much for his kindness, hospitality and for saving him

from the terrible sheep-stealers. He wanted to show his gratitude by offering the wee man whatever money he had, but the wee man had no interest in such things as money and he said to Johnny, 'If you stand in need of anything, I will give you what will keep you comfortable all your life.'

Johnny said that this was far too much and that he felt indebted to the wee man, but the wee man waved his hand at Johnny and went away for a bit and then returned with a bag full of sovereigns

and gave them to Johnny. He also gave Johnny a beautiful horse
with a saddle and bridle and told him to mount the beast.

'Don't worry' said the wee man. 'This horse will leave you right
at your destination.'

Johnny asked the wee man why he was so kind to him and the
wee man replied, ''Tis a rare thing that your kind don't help themselves to our gold without permission. You have proved yourself a
trustworthy and decent fellow, Johnny McKenna.'

With that, the wee man patted the horse and it bolted off like
a bullet. They flew across the land like the wind, clearing every
ditch, hedge and bog hole like it was not there at all. The first place
they came to was Shane Faddley's carrick, where the horse rested
for a wee bit and then they were off again. The horse then crossed
through Derrkinighbeg and Johnny could see neither ditch nor
hedge till he landed at the foot of his own garden.

When his feet touched the ground, the horse disappeared and
he walked to his front door, both pleased and honoured to have
befriended none other than the King of the Fairies!

THE SILVER DISH

*This is an old fairy tale that was told many years ago to Francis
McCarron by another Monaghan man, the late Peter McKenna of
Annahagh – and there is a fair chance that the main character in the
story was called Johnny McKenna.*

There was once a man from Co. Monaghan called Johnny
McKenna who built his house on a fairy path. Now, he was warned
by family, friends and neighbours not to build on a fairy path, but
sure, he knew better and went ahead and did it anyway.

Well, after he built his house, he and his wife moved in and all
was well until at midnight of that first night, they heard a knock
on the door. What was strange about this knock was the fact that
it seemed to come from very low down on the door, as if it was a
small child who was knocking. Now, if this was not enough, they
heard the door open and then bang shut, followed by the sound
of stomping feet on the floor. The sitting room door opened and

banged shut and all would be silent after that until the following night, when it started all over again.

Johnny McKenna and his wife got no peace at all, for the same ritual took place every night at midnight until Johnny had had enough.

So one night, Johnny went down to the sitting room, hid behind a big chair and waited to see what would happen. Well now, midnight came and, sure enough, there was a knocking on the front door and then the door opened and shut and there was the sound of thudding footsteps in the hallway and then all of a sudden the sitting room door opened and slammed shut!

Johnny could not believe his eyes, for standing there in front of him was a wee man in a green jacket, with a red cap that had a big, white owl's feather sticking out of it.

Johnny watched carefully to see what the wee man would do. He watched him walk over to the fireplace. The fire was dying down, but the smouldering embers still gave off a reddish glow. The man reached into his jacket and pulled out a wee silver dish.

Now the wee man held the silver dish up with one hand and he held the other hand right above it and he uttered these words: 'Dip the finger, not the thumb!' Then he pressed his forefinger into the middle of the dish and said, 'High away off to Scotland!' With that, he pressed his thumb into the centre of the dish and with a mighty *whooosh!*, the wee man disappeared up the chimney. Well, as you can imagine, Johnny could not believe his eyes. He was intrigued by all of this and wanted to find out more so he decided he would go down the following night to see what would happen.

Sure enough, the next night, Johnny went down to the sitting room and as soon as the clock struck midnight the front door opened and shut, there was the sound of loud footsteps and the sitting room door opened and in came the wee man, who slammed the door behind him again and went over to the fireplace. He reached into his jacket and pulled out the little dish. He held it with one hand and held the other hand right above it and uttered the same words, 'Dip the finger, not the thumb!' Then he pressed his forefinger into the middle of the dish and again he said, 'High away off to Scotland!' With that, he pressed his thumb into the centre of the dish and, with a mighty *whooosh!*, the wee man disappeared up the chimney.

At this stage Johnny was really curious and anyone who knows anything about stories will tell you that a lot things come in threes, so on the third night, Johnny decided to intervene and this is what happened …

Johnny went down to the sitting room and he moved his chair as close to the fireplace as possible before hiding behind it. As ever, the clock struck midnight and the whole procedure took place again with the wee man, who went to the fireplace and produced the silver dish. He held it with one hand, held the other hand right above it and uttered the same words, 'Dip the finger, not the thumb!'

But before he had a chance to utter another word or to put his thumb on the plate, out jumped Johnny from behind the chair. He grabbed the wee man. The fairy man disappeared in a flash and was 'gone'!

But what had he dropped on the ground? Only the little silver dish, so Johnny picked it up and looked at it for a bit. He tried to remember what the wee fairy man had done.

'Dip the finger, not the thumb!' he said, then he pressed his forefinger into the middle of the dish, but nothing happened. He tried again. 'Dip the finger, not the thumb!', he said, then he pressed his forefinger into the middle of the dish and said, 'High away off to Scotland!', but again nothing happened.

Now, Johnny was getting frustrated at this point and he thought very hard about what the fairy man had said, but then he remembered what the fairy man had done and he tried it once more.

So he said, 'Dip the finger, not the thumb!', then he pressed his forefinger into the middle of the dish and said, 'High away off to Scotland!' And with that, he remembered to dip his thumb into the centre of the dish and, with a mighty *whooosh!*, he went flying up the chimney. He went up and up into the sky and when he looked down, he saw his wee house like a speck below him. Then he started to move forward through the clouds and when he looked down, he saw farmlands, villages, towns, hills, mountains and lakes speeding by below him. Eventually, he found himself flying over cliffs and above the sea and he knew then that he was leaving the Emerald Isle behind him.

The sea was raging below him and he saw ships and sailing boats sailing along as sea birds raced around him. At last he came across more cliffs and he found himself flying over land again. He looked down below and saw lights and what looked like a big city. He felt himself starting to descend from the sky. He went down bit by bit until he found himself inside a brewery in Scotland. It was just after midnight and the whole place was locked up and there was no way out at all.

As he looked around, he saw lots and lots of crates and barrels full of beer. So he decided that while he was waiting for someone to come and open up the brewery and let him out, he would have a drink of beer, just a wee bottle … But sure, after that, he wanted another one and, as Francis McCarron once told me, having heard it himself from a man called Tom Reagan, 'The problem with drink is one is not enough, two is too much and three is not half enough.' Well, after a brave few beers, he was out like a light and slept till morning.

So the following morning, when the brewers opened up, they found a drunken Irishman out for the count, lying on the floor, surrounded by empty beer bottles.

Well, they had poor Johnny arrested for breaking and entering and theft and consumption of stolen property. Now, poor Johnny protested his innocence and tried to tell the story of how he had ended up there, but, as you can imagine, they were having none of it. They thought it was all just drunken gibberish and that he must have taken them for a pack of fools, which did not make things any better for Johnny at all. So he was taken to court, where he was sentenced to death, as theft was considered to be a terrible crime in those days.

Back then, it was also customary to grant a person a last wish before they were put to death.

Johnny's last wish was that he be allowed to kiss his wife before he died. This wish was granted. He wrote a letter home to his wife and told her all about the terrible predicament he had found himself in and he made sure to tell her to bring the wee silver dish with her. Well, luckily for Johnny, the letter arrived safely and his wife read it and, thankfully for him, she had found the wee silver dish and had kept it. So she got the boat over to Scotland and arrived on the day of Johnny's execution.

And there was her poor husband on the back of a cart being pulled by a donkey to the terrible gallows.

She went over to the cart and Johnny wrapped his arms around her and whispered in her ear, 'Did you bring the wee dish?'

'I did,' she replied and she produced the dish from under her shawl.

Johnny took it and uttered the words, 'Dip the finger, not the thumb!' Then he pressed his forefinger into the middle of the dish and said, 'High away off to Ireland!' And with that, he pressed his thumb into the centre of the dish and, with a mighty *whooosh!*, himself, his wife and even the donkey and cart were all whisked off into the sky, much to the consternation of his captors, and it was not long before he found himself outside his own wee house again.

And Peter McKenna, the man who told this tale, said that it was true for when he was a young boy, he saw Johnny McKenna collecting turf with the same ass and cart that had come with him from Scotland.

THE OLD MAN, THE OLD WOMAN AND THE LITTLE FAIRY MAN

I wrote this tale after reading a condensed version of a similar story collected by the Irish Folklore Commission Schools Collection.

There was once an old man named James O'Hagan of Drumscor, who lived in a little house on the bank of a river. It is said that the fairies used to run by his door every evening after sunset.

The old man thought he would catch one of them to see what they looked like close up. He eventually caught one of them and tied it up on the 'crane' (people hung the pots from the crane in front of the fire), so he could show his neighbours when they came into the house. The little fairy man was wearing a green suit and the tiniest shiny black shoes you ever did see and a cheeky wee grin upon his face.

A few nights later, the old man's wife was out milking the cow and when she came back into the house with the bucket of fresh milk, she tripped over a stone in the middle of the floor and spilled the milk everywhere.

It took her ages to clean the place and she even had to call on her four cats to give her a hand.

The fairy looked on, giggling and grinning.

The old woman was annoyed after tripping and falling and spilling the milk and she thought to herself that there was no good luck in the house since that chap had been tied up beside the pots.

That same evening, her husband was working beside the fairy fort in the field out the back. She started to rummage through the utensils, as though she was looking for something urgently. She was lifting iron pots and pans and metal utensils and the little fairy man was beginning to get frightened. He thought she was going to kill him. It is historically believed that fairies don't like iron or steel. It is said iron, in particular, can be used to repel, contain or harm ghosts, fairies and witches. So, the fairy man was trying to wriggle his way out of the rope that had been used to tie him to the crane.

But the old woman had no intention of harming the fairy. She untied him and watched him run as fast as he could past the cats and out the door and back up towards the fairy fort. The other little fairies were delighted to see him and asked him how he got free. As the old man was working close by, he saw and heard all of this happening and so he listened a little more closely.

The little fairy man told his friends how the old lady had tripped and fallen and then let him go free. The old man was annoyed, even angry at first, but then the little fairy man explained how the old woman had tripped over the same stone he had hidden the crock of gold under. The old man's ears pricked up and a smile was appearing on his face. He sprinted back to the house, hollering and shouting for the old woman.

When he got into the house, she was on her knees, cleaning the last of the milk she had spilt. She was quietly weeping, saying how sorry she was for letting the little fairy go.

The old man said, 'Don't worry, my true love.'

She was wondering why he was so happy. She saw a skip in his step that she hadn't seen in many a day, not since they had met at the crossroads seventy years before. He ran back outside and came in a few minutes later with a crowbar and spade.

The old lady had found herself back at that crossroads, with her floral dress and cheeks and lips red from dancing and kissing, but she was quickly awoken from her daydream.

When he came in with the crowbar and spade, she took a few steps back. Who knows? Maybe the old woman thought he had gone mad and was going to kill her and then bury her out in the field – because he was acting way out of character. First, he called her his true love and then he was skipping like a young boy with a smile on his face, a smile she didn't see all too often. Although some teeth were missing, her heart still skipped a few beats when she saw him happy and light-hearted.

But he looked at her straight in the eye and said, 'Step back, my love. I need to remove the stone in the middle of the floor.'

After a bit of difficulty and some blood, sweat and tears, the old man raised the stone and there in the middle of their floor was a crock of gold, just like the little fairy had said.

He was so pleased that the fairy folk hadn't tricked him.

The old man and the old woman sat on the floor, admiring the treasure, touching it and holding it and promising to be forever grateful.

The man stood up and threw his arms around the old woman and they lived the rest of their days secure and happy. From that day on, anyone who visited their wee house beside the river did not see a fairy, as the farmer would once have wanted – instead, they heard the story of how the fairy had left them treasure. The new-found wealth the old man and old woman had come into meant that they had the best quality of tae and cake for miles around and so the visitors came in their twos and threes over and over again to hear the story of the kind-hearted little fairy.

The old man never tried to catch a fairy ever again. Each morning, while he worked beside their fort, he would bid them good day and thank them for making life easier for him and his one true love.

WITCH WAS SHE, A WOMAN OR A HARE?

This tale was inspired by a story that was collected from Patrick Sherry, of Drumdart.

There was an old woman called Dolly Gilliland who lived on a tiny farm in Killalough around about 1887. She lived in a little hut that the locals called 'the Devil's den'.

Dolly was a character. People said she was a witch. They thought she had special powers and felt she was someone to be feared.

All that Dolly had on her land was a red hen, a donkey and two goats. Every week she would attended the farmers' market in Crocker (known then as the farmer's byre).

Every Monday morning, she would go off to the market with two pounds of butter from what little livestock she had. This wasn't much butter, but she made the trip every week nonetheless – it must have been worth her while.

People would make fun of her. Dolly was an easy target. She stood out from the crowd.

Each November, the huntsmen would be out in droves and they would taunt poor Dolly if they saw her. But on this particular day, they were more interested in catching hares and Dolly knew this, so she decided to get her own back. They saw a nice hare and were hell-bent on catching it, but the hare was swift and it was difficult to catch a hold of.

So the men set two greyhounds on it. They were close to it three or four times, but they kept missing and this made them all the more determined to catch this particular hare. No one was going to get the better of those men. The two greyhounds couldn't even get near the hare, so the men sent for a famous black greyhound that lived in Co. Tyrone.

On a bright May morning, the famous black greyhound was set upon the hare. The hare went skipping through the spring flowers and he would rise five feet off the ground every time the black greyhound went near it. The hare moved fast. It approached Dolly's hut and just as it was crossing the threshold of the half-door, the dog caught the hare and bit the poor animal, but it got inside just in time, before the black greyhound was able to finish the job.

The men following behind heard the cry from the hare and ran towards the hut and found the dog outside with blood around its mouth.

When the men looked over the half-door, the old woman was sitting by the fire and her leg was bleeding. The old woman said, 'Yiz have a nice pup,' and one man said back to her, 'It's nearly too nice for you.'

Was Dolly a witch? Did she turn into a hare and make fun of the men? Or did they just take a dislike to Dolly? Maybe the greyhound bit Dolly and the men didn't see, but it makes a better story to say that she had turned into a hare and then back into Dolly. Either way, it's a great tale.

The Fairy Field

When I was interviewing people in Inniskeen, I met up with Patsy and Linda Boylan. They were kind enough to take myself and my partner Paula to see their fairy field and the fairy fort that stands upon it. And this is a wee story about it …

Well, Patsy drove us right into the fairy field, which had an unusual and strange atmosphere about it. He told us that many people who went into the field by themselves at night could not get out of it at all. He spoke of one man who had spent the whole night trying to get out only to find that there were no openings and every hedge and ditch was too high or too deep to get out of. He couldn't escape until the following morning.

He also spoke of a friend called Willy Shields, now in his mid-seventies, who, when he was a young man, was coming home from a dance and decided to take a shortcut through Patsy's field. He came into the field from a place called Tallans' Corner, but poor Willy couldn't get out again and found himself trapped inside the field till the following morning, by which time he was totally exhausted and bewildered.

Patsy then told us that back in the late 1950s, there was a man called Peter Martin who had a wee plot on Patsy's field where he